# Healing the Wounds that Divide Us

The Seven Mysteries of Ethical Decision

# Healing the Wounds that Divide Us

## The Seven Mysteries of Ethical Decision

# Thomas Alonso Massey

VISION QUEST BOOKS
San Diego

HEALING THE WOUNDS THAT DIVIDE US

Vision Quest Books/November 1995

All rights reserved.
Copyright © 1995 by Thomas Alonso Massey

No part of this book may be reproduced or transmitted in any form or by any means, electronic or mechanical, including photocopying, recording, or by any information storage and retrieval system, without the permission in writing from the publisher.
For information address: Vision Quest Books

Healing the Wounds that Divide Us
by Thomas Alonso Massey
ISBN 1-887607-01-3

Set in 12 pt. Roman

---

Vision Quest Books, 524 Reisling Terrace, Chula Vista, California 91913. Call (619) 482-4280 for information.

---

PRINTED IN CANADA
PUBLISHED IN THE UNITED STATES OF AMERICA

RRH 0 9 8 7 6 5 4 3 2

To My Wife Gabrielle Alonso Massey

For her great love and support and to all the men of the Unitarian Universalist Men's Fellowship, for their courage, openess and guidance.

## ACKNOWLEDGMENT

The foundation for my great interest in ethics and values lies in the loving care and excellent example provided by my parents, Thomas and Elizabeth Massey. My father's keen and sensitive interest in the truth led me ultimately to major in philosophy and to study law, while always honoring the importance of religion. My mother set the stage to endeavor to fulfill the Christian concept of love in our everyday lives.

Reverend Burton Smith has been a spiritual father and mentor to guide me over the years after my father's death. I owe to him my fullest understanding of what love is and how it must play a role in every part of our lives and social institutions, especially the criminal justice system.

In recent years, my spiritual strength and inspiration has been with the Unitarian Church and foremost with the men of the Unitarian Universalist Men's Fellowship of San Diego, California. Although all of these men have counted immeasurably in my life, I would particularly like to thank those who assisted me with their advice and support in the drafting of this manuscript. Reverend Tom Owen-Towle shared both his time and insights on the overall concept of the book and the philosophic analysis. Dr. Richard Wilkie graciously provided guidance in both organization and style. Dr. Wilkie inspired the final master theme and explication of the Seven Mysteries that guided me to my final conclusions. Dr. Ken Helfant reviewed the text from the standpoint of a practicing clinical psychologist. Dr. John P. Kinney contributed valuable insight from a criminological perspective to the chapters on criminal justice. And conversations with my dear friends Jim Faris and Ross Porter helped me clarify many of the insights I had been seeking.

My writing has been profoundly inspired and supported by many members of what is collectively called the men's movement. Starting in the order in which I have met them, I am indebted to Shepherd Bliss for the excellent introduction to the world of mythology and poetry when his traveling band created a spiritual workshop in San Diego. The leaders of the 1993 Men's

Leadership Conference in Mendocino, California, also made a powerful impact on me and this work. I am especially thankful to Robert Bly for the opportunity to test my belief in front of 120 men that "evil" really does not "exist," but is merely the absence of love. And I am greatly appreciative of the kind assistance and support given by Allan B. Chinen, M.D., for both his encouragement and corroboration in excerpts from his book, *Once Upon a Midlife*.

My special gratitude goes to my legal secretary, LaTonya Torian, for her faithful and tireless typing of countless versions of the manuscript during the past two years.

This project was also made possible by the excellent and dedicated work of Patricia Godsoe, who prepared the layout of the text and Steven Fellwock, who arranged the final layout, printing, distribution and marketing.

My greatest support and dedication has come from Gabrielle, who has supported this work not only as a loving wife and friend, but in its editing, securing permissions to print, and marketing. Without her patience and encouragement, this work would not have been possible.

Thomas Alonso Massey

# Healing the Wounds that Divide Us

## The Seven Mysteries of Ethical Decision

# CONTENTS

Acknowledgments   vii
A Personal Note To The Reader   xiv

## PART ONE
## THE MYSTERY OF ETHICAL DECISION

The Need For Mystery In An Age Of Intolerance   3
    Three Ethical Dilemmas   4

## PART TWO
## THE SEVEN MYSTERIES OF ETHICAL DECISION

Mystery Number 1:
The Only Rule...Is That There Are No Rules!   9
    Liberal And Conservative Hypocrisies   11
    Rules Versus Results   13

Mystery Number 2:
The Broader The Truth, The More Impractical It Is!   17

Mystery Number 3:
Everyone's Needs Are Equally Important   21

Mystery Number 4:
Ethical Decisions Are Made By People, Not Robots!   25
    The Person   26
    Applying Our Principles To The "Facts"   29

Mystery Number 5:
"Evil" Is Dead!   35
    The Perils Of "Either-or-ism"   35
    Snow White Without A Witch   42

The Search For Evil   44
A Guided Ethical Mediation   45
The "Blame Game" Is Over   48
The Resurrection Of The "Blame Game"   52
The Wisdom Of Old Age   57

**Mystery Number 6:**
**Identical Acts Of Force May Be Ethical Or Unethical   61**
　Struck Down By Love?   64
　Shipwrecked   67
　Why People Hate Lawyers   71
　America's Addiction To The Wicked Witch   73

**Mystery Number 7:**
**We Are, Paradoxically, Both Responsible And Nonresponsible For Our Actions   79**

PART THREE
# THE SEVEN MYSTERIES AND THE ETHICAL DILEMMAS OF OUR AGE

Abortion: The Ultimate Ethical Dilemma   87
　Can There Be An Absolute Rule Regarding Abortions?   88
　Balancing The Rights And Needs Of The Mother, The Fetus And Society   93
　Who Must Make The Decision?   95
　Should The Father Have Any Say?   98
　Abortion As Neither "Good" Nor "Evil"   100
　The Ethical Validity Of The Use Of Force In Abortion   101
　Abortion And Personal Responsibility   102
　The Continuing Ethical Validity Of *Roe Versus Wade* And Later Supreme Court Cases   104

Criminal Justice and The Death Penalty:
The Ultimate Separation From Society   109
　Separation As Punishment   110
　Criminal Sentences Must Be Based On Both The Facts And The Person...Not Absolute Rules   113
　The Human Urge For Revenge   118

Sentencing To Balance The Needs Of Society And The Needs Of
  The Criminal    120
The Ethical Use Of Ultimate Force: The Death Penalty    123
Execution by lightning?    128
The Execution of Robert Alton Harris    130
An Alternative To The Death Penalty    134
The Jury System On Trial:
  The Menendez Brothers    139
  O.J. Simpson    141
The Heroic Death...Is Dead! 143
The Spring of 1995: The Confessions Of McNamara And The
  Apprehension of McVeigh    148

Death In America:
The American Ideal Death: "Keep Both Guns Blasting Till You
Go Down!"    153
  Can There Be An Absolute Rule Dictating How We All
    Must Die?    154
  The Necessity For Guidelines    156
  The Individual, Not The State, Should Determine The Terms Of
    Our Deaths    158
  There Is No Good Or Bad Way To Die    160
  Force As Part Of Our Final Action    162
  Is The Right To Die Guaranteed By The Constitution?    165

## CONCLUSION:

The Rewards Of Ethical Mysticism—Control, Toleration And
Freedom    169

## ADDENDUM:

Legislative Blueprint For The Future    173

# A Personal Note To The Reader

Something in me cries out to make this a more loving, tolerant and understanding world. That same spirit must be within you, the reader, as well. We have more than enough physical suffering from the natural world: earthquakes, fires, floods, famine and disease. What we do not need is to add to our suffering by the ignorance, intolerance and hypocrisy that leads to our killing each other in the name of justice, whether it be local, national or international justice.

If we are to put an end to the suffering which we cause ourselves, we must know and fully understand ethics and moral reasoning. I believe that, as in many other areas, the more we come to understand ethics and moral reasoning, the more we will realize we cannot always predict moral decisions. We must realize that there is a mysterious quality to the realm of ethics that defies our childlike desire to cling to simplistic answers and rigid rules. In short, the more we understand about ethics, the more we will marvel at what we cannot know about it. Let us begin to explore these many mysteries together, for, if we do, we will naturally generate a nation of wonder, appreciation, love and tolerance.

My questioning of the established moral order began at a very early age. Perhaps it did for you as well? When you were a child, did you ever wonder if you had committed the "one unforgivable sin?" As a young boy raised in a strict Presbyterian home, I wondered with fear and amazement from the beginning about such questions of right and wrong, good and evil. What, after all, was this "one unforgivable sin?" I can still sense the great anxiety of not knowing what the one unforgivable sin was and, therefore, with childhood logic, not knowing whether I had committed it or not! This was extremely serious business, since, if you had committed it, you would, by definition, go to "hell"...no matter what! My departure from this strict Presbyterian upbringing came not without much resolution of guilt and fear, as well as building of moral and ethical self confidence. I have come to believe that fashioning and creating our moral identity is as vital as the creation of every other aspect of our lives.

My ethical wanderings and personal journey have taken me all over the world. After majoring in philosophy at the College of William and Mary, I joined the Peace Corps and served two years as an English teacher in the Ivory Coast, West Africa. Thereafter, I studied at the University of Virginia School of Law. Upon graduation, I volunteered to serve as a Navy lawyer on board the *USS MIDWAY*, home ported in Yokosuka, Japan. During five and a half years of active duty, I tried hundreds of cases, including charges of rape, attempted murder and felony drug sales.

After I resigned from the Navy in 1980, I left the world of criminal litigation for that of civil litigation. First, I became an attorney for an insurance defense law firm in San Diego, California. Two years later, I opened my own practice, emphasizing personal injury cases from the plaintiff's stand-point. I discovered there is a silent war going on at all times between these two groups, the plaintiff's bar and the insurance industry's lawyers. My conflicting feelings about how this system works will be brought out as I discuss the application of the "fault system" to our legal system.

I have also practiced family law, medical and legal malpractice, military law and general litigation since opening my own office. This variety has kept me intellectually fascinated with the law and it also has given me a sense of perspective for the future of our legal system. The numerous stages in this journey have afforded me a perspective on both the law and ethics that I do not feel I could otherwise have reached. My evolution through the Peace Corps, Navy JAGC Corps and now civil litigation seems, in hindsight, to have been a natural journey. Along the way I have come to realize that no one person or group of people has a monopoly on the world of ethics; in fact, the theme of this book is that the opposite is true. The realm of ethics is not a world of absolutes; rather, it contains endless paths with equally magnificent and worthy views, to be selected by each of us at every stage of our journeys. In Part One, I set forth why we as a nation greatly need such a vision of ethics and morality.

The realm of ethics is one of mystery and, by "mystery," I mean initially unknowable. However, to honor the mystery of ethics is not to say we can never understand what we do when we make ethical decisions. We can at least understand the process of ethical decision and therefore journey into this realm with some navigational aids to chart our course and location. If we cannot prove that there are only certain courses to be chosen, at least we can show how people choose a certain ethical path and how we have developed our ethical thinking. In Part Two, I examine seven of the dynamics of ethical thinking, which I have labeled mysteries, since each one treats an unknowable and unpredictable aspect of ethical thinking. These seven mysteries of ethical decision making are these dynamics of both ethical reasoning and conduct that, in everyday terms, describe both how we make ethical decisions and why ethical decisions cannot be programmed in advance, to be obeyed without exception by all other peoples.

In Part Three, the seven mysteries are applied to three areas of ethical debate in which our nation seems to be most evenly and at times violently divided: abortion, the death penalty, and death with dignity. I am mindful that others have written on each of these topics in greater detail and with greater authority. I have no interest in providing scholarly analysis in each of these issues. My "bliss," in the words of Joseph Campbell, and therefore my contribution, is to see the forest and not the trees—the broad, general ethical principles that apply to all of these seemingly unresolvable ethical questions. I have deliberately written in a personal manner—as one individual seeking what truths may be found in these ethically troubling times. This, then, is a book written by one reaching out to his fellow ethical wanderers. It is a call to common sense in a tumultuous, divisive era in our country's moral history. Let us begin our journey together.

*Theodore Gericault,* The Raft of the "Madusa." *1818-19*

*Like these sailors adrift, our ethical journeys are always, at first, into the unkown.*

#  Part One

## The Mystery of Ethical Decision

# THE NEED FOR MYSTERY IN AN AGE OF INTOLERANCE

In 1861, our nation exploded in civil war over questions of power, economic control and the ethical issue of slavery. Over 600,000 American men lost their lives in this struggle; more of our men were killed than in World War I, World War II, the Korean Conflict and the Vietnam wars combined.[1] Today, with the fall of Communism and with no common enemy to fight, we seem to be turning to ourselves once again to find our enemies. We are now confronting a civil war over life-and-death ethical issues. Divided on the fundamental ethical issues of abortion, the death penalty, and death with dignity, we are wounding ourselves anew with accusations of the wrongness and the evil of opposing viewpoints. There is no clear understanding or acceptance of any of these issues, and each side is desperately fearful that the other side's view will ultimately prevail.

We have spokespeople such as Rush Limbaugh condemning the rate of abortions at one and a half million per year for the past twenty years as being tantamount to 30 million murders! Others have murdered doctors involved in the termination of pregnancies. Yet, the majority favors the woman's right to choose abortion. Consequently, President Bush's stand against a woman's right to choose probably cost him the 1992 presidential election.

In the case of criminal justice and the death penalty, a clear majority of the people are in favor of the death penalty; yet when it comes to actually imposing the death penalty, virtually no one is executed, so that its imposition becomes a matter of sheer accident! For example, since 1977 when California restored capital punishment, 328 people are facing death row; yet only two have been executed.[2] Throughout the nation, more than 2,600 individuals are on death row, but only about 30 have been executed in any year since 1976, leading one commentator to write that death row inmates have a far greater likelihood of dying from illness or old age than from the actual carrying out of the death penalty.[3]

Finally, on the question of euthanasia, the majority favors individual control and death with dignity as to when and how a person will die; yet initiatives allowing for such choice were defeated by narrow margins recently in the states of Washington and California. In 1994 however, a euthanasia statute was passed in Oregon, making it the first state in America to permit physicians to prescribe lethal medication for terminally ill people.

Ethically, our nation is undergoing a great evolution, and, as we did in our Civil War, we are suffering great turmoil and strife in the process. Although our ethical age calls for understanding, toleration and acceptance, we are beset with extremist views, both liberal and conservative, that tend only to wound our people more deeply. It is time for all of us to take a long, hard look at where ethical beliefs come from and how we came to think the way we do. How is it, for example, that the nation seems to be so closely divided on these three issues? Why do we think and believe the way we do on these issues? Perhaps if you and I can understand how we came to believe the way we do, we will also understand why others oppose our beliefs so vehemently.

## Three Ethical Dilemmas

Let us take a look at three imaginary cases, to present the complexity and difficulty of the ethical decision making that we will be considering.

Case One: Julie defies her parents, gets drunk one evening and becomes pregnant by her boyfriend. He is a heavy drug user.

Neither has finished high school and neither has a job or any job skills. Julie is fearful and depressed. They are too young and immature to handle marriage, much less the responsibilities of raising a child. Yet they both are consumed with guilt over the thought of an abortion, and they had dreamed of one day getting married and having children.

Case Two: Richard robs and then ruthlessly executes two teenage boys after locking them in the trunk of their car. Later, he callously eats a hamburger the boys had purchased just before the attack. The jury is called upon to decide whether this crime deserves the death penalty. Their task is not easy: Richard himself had been the victim of terrible sexual and psychological abuse, having been born into a world of drug addiction and brutality and abandoned by his parents.

Case Three: Howard, age 75, faces terminal cancer and is told by his doctor that the pain will become worse, and that he will lose all control over his mind. The cost for continued treatment will reach astronomical amounts, depleting all that he has saved for his spouse and children. He has lived his whole life with compassion and resourcefulness, always setting a good example for his children. He is torn between his desire to make his last days on earth beautiful and meaningful for him and his loved ones...and his survival instinct to fight to the finish.

The individuals in these three cases face painful and difficult dilemmas. In each case, they find themselves caught between many conflicting goals and sets of values. They are in true ethical dilemmas, to be resolved only by their own ethical journey. In the case involving a jury, twelve individuals must miraculously blend their thinking into a unanimous verdict. These are, ultimately, decisions that no one can make for them. In fact, imposing a decision on them would take away the personal integrity and meaning of their lives! And, as we will explore later, personal decision is an inherent part of all ethical decisions.

The greatness of our American government is our long-fought-for and cherished freedom of the individual to make such profound personal choices. Our present challenge is to avoid the temptation of the majority to impose its will on everyone else: that is, to take away individual ethical decision making. Either by direct law or by moral condemnation, we are condemning people whose lives do not fit into our concept of "normalcy."

Our nation is racked with self-destruction and pain over these ethical issues. I have viewed with great sorrow the strife that our nation's ethical conflict has produced. The national furor over these three life-and-death issues has manifested in illegal picketing, violent demonstrations, hate crimes and, recently, the tragic death of two medical physicians who performed abortions. This book is dedicated to ending that strife, not by merely calling for peace and toleration, but through understanding of the ethical process.

My message is simple: the realm of ethics is inherently indeterminate and it contains an indefinite number of solutions. It consists of principles and truths that exist concurrently as a whole, and with equal force and power. As Neils Bohr has said, "The opposite of a fact is a falsehood, but the opposite of one great truth is another great truth."[4] Furthermore, these principles or truths are of no practical use or significance until individuals, with all their wounds and needs, attempt to apply them to their particular situations. In other words, principles must be applied by individuals to individual cases. They should not be imposed by the state as a set of precise rules. Once we have understood that, we as individuals and as a nation may begin to appreciate other people's decisions and other people's points of view. Such toleration of others also provides the simultaneous blessing of individual control of our own lives. This is the understanding that will lead our nation forward in its ethical evolution.

# Part Two

## The Seven Mysteries Of Ethical Decision

# Mystery Number 1

# The Only Rule... Is That There Are No Rules!

> When I was a child, I talked like a child,
> I thought like a child, I reasoned like a child.
> When I became a man, I put childish ways behind me.
>
> 1 Corinthians 13:11

> The golden rule...is that there are no golden rules.
>
> George Bernard Shaw, *Maxims for Revolutionists*

What does it mean to *think* like a child? In part, it means wanting everyone else to do exactly what you like to do. Has a small child ever come to you, insisting that you try whatever they are eating or that you play exactly what they are playing? On such occasions, I have been struck by the neediness of the child to get me not only to do but also to enjoy precisely what the child is enjoying! At an *adult* level, this need transforms to wanting everyone else to think just as we think and to believe exactly what we believe. This childish behavior is reflected all too often in adults when we say, "Not only will you do what I say, you will like it!" If our childhood wound was never being allowed to think for ourselves, we may sadly impose such rigidity on all those around us! The tragic example of the religious fanatic David Koresh comes to mind. Koresh was the ultimate fanatic—he wanted people not only to believe in him, but to be willing to die for him. He ended by coercing his followers to suicide in the fiery inferno of the Waco, Texas, compound. On the other hand, we may lead our lives in constant rebellion against all rules and authority. Although most of us do not fall prey to such extremes, even the most mature of us prefer to surround ourselves with those who think just as we do and who act just as we do.

At a social and national level, our childish clamoring for agreement manifests itself in the creation of "absolute rules." The problem, of course, with absolute rules is that they are often absolutely wrong in specific situations. In fact, the only absolute rule...is that there can be no absolute rules!

If our first and most pervasive mystery of ethics appears preposterous, let me take just a few examples to explain what I mean. The *Old Testament* set forth in the Ten Commandments absolute rules, which from their inception were destined to be broken on occasion. Take for example, the proscription, "Thou shalt not kill." No one really believes that killing is always unethical; otherwise, every war that the United States has ever fought would be ethically unjustified. We would not then have had a basis to fight the Nazi campaign against the Jews in World War II, nor would it have been ethical if Hitler had been assassinated. Yet virtually everyone would agree that the assassination of Hitler would have been morally justified.

The Old Testament also flatly prohibits adultery, but it doesn't take much imagination to conceive of an espionage situation where adultery might be committed for one's country. And, in fact, the famous author and religious leader, Dr. Scott Peck, once stated in his landmark work, *The Road Less Traveled,* that he would engage in sex with a patient if that were the only way to reach a desired therapeutic goal.

"Thou shalt not steal," another ancient proscription, sets forth a clearly valid general rule; yet, on the other hand, who would not steal food if that were the only way to preserve one's life or the lives of one's family? In short, there is probably no such thing as an ethical rule that cannot be broken in the name of adherence to an even higher principle, such as the overall good of the people. Inevitably, then, the creation of inflexible ethical rules in contemporary politics leads to all sorts of hypocrisy and untenable positions, as we shall see.

## LIBERAL AND CONSERVATIVE HYPOCRISIES

Consider the apparent hypocrisy of "flaming liberals" and "arch conservatives" on the three issues of abortion, capital punishment and death with dignity. Flaming liberals think it's acceptable to kill helpless fetuses, but not to kill heinous criminals. The same liberals would also readily adopt a system allowing terminally ill patients to choose death with dignity. For them, life seems to be sacred only for criminals.

On the other hand, for "arch conservatives" it's acceptable to kill heinous criminals, but it's never acceptable to kill an unwanted fetus destined to become an addicted criminal. The same conservatives would also reject the freedom to choose to end one's own life during a terminal illness. For them, life seems to be sacred only for the unborn and the very sick or old.

On the next page is a graph depicting visually what might be called the "sacredness" factor. The vertical column indicates the amount of sacredness or value given during a human life. The horizontal column indicates passage of time from childhood to middle age to old age. The two curves represent the so-called *conservative* v. *liberal* viewpoints. If this graph strikes you as somewhat ridiculous, then it has already served its purpose!

Under the "conservative curve," a fetus is marked as absolutely sacred, but a mature adult's life is expendable and subject ultimately to the death penalty for extreme misconduct. Then, suddenly life becomes sacred again in old age, because you are not allowed to relieve yourself of the agonies of a terminal illness under any condition. It seems that for such people, life appears to be sacred only at its beginning and end.

# Liberal And Conservative Hypocrisies

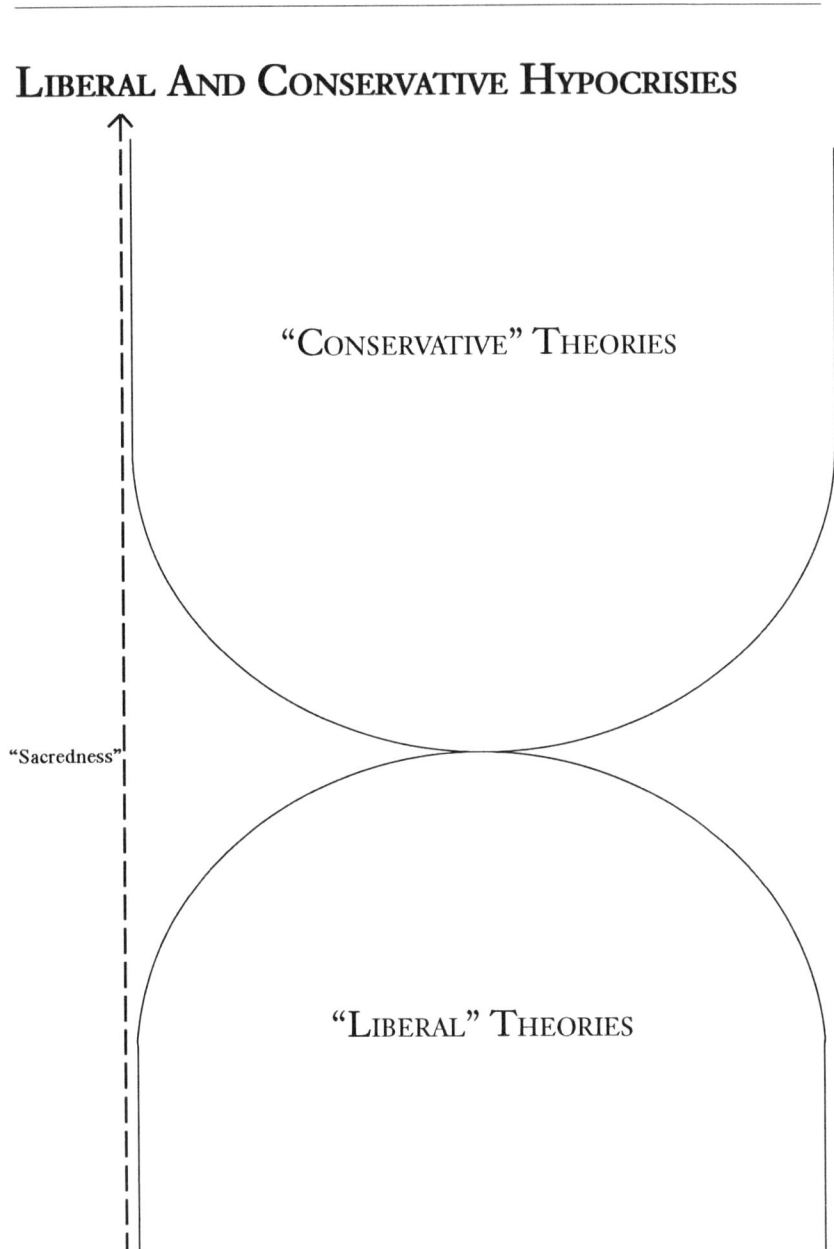

Under the "liberal curve," the fetus' life is expendable for the welfare of the living, but once a person is alive and reaches adulthood, his or her life is sacred and can not be taken by the state regardless of the person's extreme criminal misconduct. Finally, those facing terminal illnesses are allowed to end their own lives gracefully according to their informed and ultimate wishes. It would appear for such liberals, life is sacred only for those within middle age.

Obviously, however, the sacredness and value of life should not depend on one's age. For example, a 22-year-old's life is certainly no more valuable than a 44-year-old person's life. Nevertheless, extremist conservative and liberal views create the inconsistency that life at one end of the spectrum is more worthy or more to be protected than at the other end. However, although the value of life remains constant through age, we all have to make decisions at some points in our lives to end either our lives or the lives of others. Though we might wish it were not true, there are simply no rules telling us how to make these decisions.

## RULES VERSUS RESULTS

Philosophers have debated for centuries whether our ethics should be controlled by strict adherence to rules or fashioned by the totality of circumstances in which the individual finds himself. This might be characterized as the "rules versus results" debate, or, in more ethically technical language, the "deontological versus teleological" debate. People who promote pre-existing rules are criticized as strict absolutists, allowing for none of the complex personal considerations and relative circumstances in which a person may find himself. On the other hand, people who ignore rules, the so-called "ethical relativists," are criticized for allowing too much individual freedom of choice so that, whatever a person chooses, is right. In an extreme view, they believe "there is nothing either good or bad but thinking makes it so," to borrow Shakespeare's phrase for Hamlet. This, arguably, destroys the very concept of right and wrong. However, you do not have to be an ethical "rocket scientist" to understand that either extreme fails to afford the maximum potential for arriving at ethical decisions.

As an overview, here are the extreme positions applied to our three principal areas of concern.

| Ethical Issue | Inflexible Rules Approach | Individual Choice Approach |
|---|---|---|
| | Philosophical Basis: Human Responsibility | Philosophical Basis: Human Freedom |
| Abortion | Fetus always protected; choice to abort never allowed. | Women can choose to abort fetus at anytime for any reason. |
| Death penalty | Death penalty mandatory in certain cases. | Death penalty imposed randomly...or abolished. |
| Death with dignity for terminally ill | No one allowed to choose manner and time of death. | Each individual may choose death whenever they see fit, regardless of their condition. |

The way these columns have been created, obviously either extreme position restricts the greatest potential for ethical decision making. Under the "Inflexible Rules" column, the philosophy promoted is that rules and mere existence are sacred and that there should be no death of any kind whatsoever except that imposed by "Mother Nature" or by society to punish certain crimes. This allows for little control by individuals over their lives or for individual control by society over its members.

On the other hand, taken to the extreme, the "Individual Choice" column condones such reckless and unchecked freedom by the individual that great havoc and injury to human life could occur. Realistically, although individual choice and control over people's lives are obviously necessary for an ethically conscious life, if individual choices were not circumscribed by some set of pre-existing guidelines, our society would, from a moral standpoint, descend into ethical anarchy. Thus, while principles are indispensable, rules can destroy freedom of choice. In short, we need both principles and freedom to apply those principles as we individually see fit.

In contemporary political debate and thought, politicians are warned they cannot "straddle" such issues. He or she must choose—perhaps to their political peril—one of the extremes on this ethical continuum. Politicians are told that they must either be pro-choice or pro-life and that there is nothing in between. They must be either for the death penalty or against it. Finally, they must either be for or against the right of a terminally ill individual to choose a dignified death. We are in fact being "either-or'ed" to death, as President Clinton once phrased it. And, if you cannot make up your mind, "once and for all," you are accused of the worst of all political ills..."waffling," even though we might all agree that even a waffle has two sides!

In our ethical journey together, we will discover that there is an infinity of ethical truths that exist somewhere in between the extremes of absolutism and relativism. Once we have realized this ethical reality, our task becomes to create institutions and legal/moral guidelines that allow the individual to decide, or be judged, by reasonable ethical principles and by reference to the relative circumstances of each person's life. We must constantly balance our ethical lives between conflicting principles, because, as Somerset Maugham phrased it, the path to salvation is as narrow...as a razor's edge.

# Mystery Number 2

# The Broader The Truth, The More Impractical It Is!

*And now these three remain: Faith, hope and love
But the greatest of these is love.*

1 Corinthians 13

If we have no absolute rules to guide us in each and every situation, what then? We obviously must turn to ethical principles to guide us in our ethical lives, but we immediately run into another ethical dilemma: the broader the ethical principle, the less practical it is! In other words, the more believable or irrefutable the ethical principle, the less it tells us exactly what to do in our everyday lives.

We have seen that "thou shalt not kill, commit adultery or steal" are absolute rules that must somehow or other mysteriously give way to the higher authority of a greater principle when the circumstances require it. What, then, is that greater principle? The most beautiful, profound and traditionally accepted highest ethical principle is, of course, that of love. The concept of love is surely one in which everyone believes. At least, few would disagree with it. But what does it mean? In any given ethical dilemma, doing the most "loving" thing could easily mean ten different things to ten different people. And it is usually impossible to convince someone else that your interpretation of the most loving thing to do is the best interpretation. Consider another compelling principle discovered by Albert Schweitzer, the famous theologian, musician and medical missionary. In his autobiography, *Out of My Life and Thought,* he describes a magical moment of clarification reached during a long river journey to visit a fellow missionary. For years he had been struggling to resolve his conflict between the material world and the spiritual world. His personal struggle reminds us of the individuality of each person's ethical journey:

> In undertaking this I seemed to myself to be like a man who has to build a new and better boat to replace a rotten one in which he can no longer venture to trust himself to the sea, and yet does not know how to begin.
> 
> For months on end I lived in a continual state of mental excitement. Without the least success I let my thinking be concentrated, even all through my daily work at the hospital, on the real nature of the affirmative attitude and of ethics, and on the question of what they have in common. I was wandering about in a thicket in which no path was to be found. I was leaning with all my might against an iron door which would not yield.

Then, suddenly, he was graced by a profound insight that came to him after several days on a steamer:

> Slowly we crept upstream, laboriously feeling—it was the dry season—for the channels between the sandbanks. Lost in thought I sat on the deck of the barge, struggling to find the elementary and universal conception of the ethical which I had not discovered in any philosophy. Sheet after sheet I covered with disconnected sentences, merely to

keep myself concentrated on the problem. Late on the third day, at the very moment when, at sunset, we were making our way through a herd of hippopotamuses, there flashed upon my mind, unforeseen and unsought, the phrase, "Reverence for Life." The iron door had yielded: the path in the thicket had become so visible. Now I had found my way to the idea in which affirmation of the world and ethics are contained side by side! Now I knew that the ethical acceptance of the world and of life, together with the ideals of civilization contained in this concept, has a foundation in thought.

Schweitzer's compelling ethic, Reverence for Life, includes not only the need to respect the needs of other humans and animals, but ultimately the need to respect one's own personal needs and the needs of society as well:

Affirmation of life is the spiritual act by which man ceases to live unreflectively and begins to devote himself to his life with reverence in order to raise it to its true value. To affirm life is to deepen, to make more inward, and to exalt the will-to-life.

At the same time the man who has become a thinking being feels a compulsion to give to every will-to-life the same reverence for life that he gives to his own. He experiences that other life in his own. He accepts as being good: to preserve life, to promote life, to raise to its highest value life which is capable of development; and as being evil: to destroy life, to injure life, to repress life which is capable of development. This is the absolute, fundamental principle of the moral, and it is a necessity of thought.

> The great fault of all ethics hitherto has been that they believed themselves to have to deal only with the relations of man to man. In reality, however, the question is what is his attitude to the world and all life that comes within his reach. A man is ethical only when life, as such, is sacred to him, that of plants and animals as that of his fellow men, and when he devotes himself helpfully to all life that is in need of help.[5]

Perhaps the concept of reverence for life provides more guidance than the more general concept of love, since it describes an affirmative approach to promoting and preserving all living creatures. However, this concept suffers similarly in its application to daily life. Unfortunately, the concept of "reverence for life" will not likely provide anyone with definitive answers to the questions that we are addressing: abortion, the death penalty and death with dignity. Obviously, people on opposite extremes of these ethical issues claim that only their position promotes the greatest preservation of life. For example, a pro-life activist would argue that only the protection of all fetuses preserves and reveres life. But a pro-choice proponent would say that reverence for life requires bringing into this world only children who can actually be loved and nurtured.

Similarly, a pro-death penalty proponent would argue that only imposition of the death penalty can preserve and protect the life of the common public; whereas, a person opposed to the death penalty would say that reverence for life requires preserving the life of even the most heinous murderer. In the end, then, we find an insurmountable problem with such profound truths as "love" and "reverence for life": while we may all believe in them, we can never agree on what they mean when it comes to a particular issue or set of circumstances. However, once we fully comprehend this ethical reality, we will be one step closer to a society of ethical compassion and toleration.

# MYSTERY NUMBER 3

## EVERYONE'S NEEDS ARE EQUALLY IMPORTANT.

*You have heard that it was said,
"Eye for eye, and tooth for tooth."
But I tell you, do not resist an evil person.
If someone strikes you on the right cheek,
turn to him the other also.*

5 Matthew 38

No one in their right mind really believes in "turning the other cheek" if that means that it is O.K. to hurt oneself or allow oneself to be hurt physically or emotionally. First of all, allowing someone to hurt you physically is masochism. It is clearly recognized as a form of mental illness that destroys both the victim and the perpetrator. As the saying goes, "If there were no sheep there would be no wolves." Allowing oneself to be hurt emotionally can be equally harmful. One development of this thinking is the concept of codependency: if you are allowing yourself to be emotionally dominated by another person, such that you have no identity, individuality or goals of your own, you are helping neither yourself nor that other person. It is unlikely that Christ was referring to such masochism or codependence when he spoke about "turning the other cheek." The concept was undoubtedly a moral breakthrough, as it was probably stated in extreme contrast to the "kill or be killed" mentality of that age. It was indeed a breakthrough in moral reasoning to conceive that helping other people and being of service to other people is a more worthwhile life than controlling, overpowering or manipulating other people.

Of course, an ethical life rejects both abuse or harm to oneself as well as to others. Ethical conduct always considers the needs of all people concerned. The problem, however, is that all people's needs are equally important, and there are no fixed and ready answers when people's needs conflict. Ethical "reality" then, is to be found mysteriously somewhere between asserting our own needs and recognizing the needs of others. It is a mystery and unknowable because our needs and the needs of others are constantly changing. It is also a mystery because it is difficult to know at any given time whether turning our attention to our own needs is more appropriate than focusing on the needs of others. One thing is clear, however: we must constantly balance our present and future needs against the needs of those around us, as well as against the needs within our larger society.

The classical Christian concept of love as turning the other cheek must be tempered with our modern and practical understanding of the interdependence of all people. Indeed, even Christ admonished His followers to be "as wise as a serpent and gentle as a lamb." As an example, then, of this newer understanding, I would interpret the Apostle Paul's famous letter to the Corinthians on love with the following expansion for our age:

| PAUL'S VERSION | 20th CENTURY VERSION |
|---|---|
| Love is patient, love is kind. | Love is either patient or impatient as circumstances require. Love will use all necessary force to achieve what is best for all concerned in the end. |
| It does not envy, it does not boast, it is not proud. | Love encourages every human to reach their greatest potential and to be proud of everyone's accomplishments, including one's own. |
| It is not rude, it is not self-seeking, it is not easily angered, it keeps no record of wrongs. | Love seeks the good of others along with one's own welfare. It expresses anger to reveal one's needs and beliefs without attacking others. It remembers injuries only to prevent hurt in the future. |
| Love does not delight in evil but rejoices in the truth. | Love delights in each person's truth and accepts both each person's infinite power to love and infinite need for love. |
| It always protects, always trusts, always hopes, always perseveres. | Love protects oneself to be able to nurture others. Love trusts and hopes for the best in others, but lets go of others when they can destroy you. |
| Love never fails. | No one is fully loving or fully unloving. Everyone has the same capacity to love and need to be loved, but one's needs and capacities vary infinitely from time to time, from the total power to love to the total need to be loved. |

We will apply this expanded concept of love in all of the ethical considerations that follow.

For example, in the death penalty issue, love requires consideration of both the protection of society and the recognition of a murderer's individual humanity. On the issue of abortion, love requires consideration of both a mother's capacity to care for a child and the right of a developed fetus to come into existence. Finally, on the question of the right to death with dignity, love must weigh the excruciating pain of a terminal illness against society's need to protect and preserve the lives of the sick and elderly. How and by what institutional means these decisions should be made is the scope and challenge of this book.

Before we leave the subject of love, let us consider the order in which love comes. I believe that love of ourselves is indeed more primary than love of others. This is simply because we can not love others until we first love ourselves. This is not to say that love of oneself is better or more important, only that love of oneself is first in time, even though the love of oneself invariably leads to love of others. I stress this because the most difficult thing we humans do is to love ourselves, whether it be by accepting the love of others or, more powerfully, accepting the love of our God. In my own life, my most terrifying and exhilarating moments have been those when pure love was offered to me. The terror comes from having to realize that one is indeed worth loving. The exhilaration is the joy of spontaneously sharing that love once received.

# Mystery Number 4

# Ethical Decisions Are Made By People, Not Robots!

> *I early arrived at the insight that when no answer comes from within to the problems and complexities of life, they ultimately mean very little.*
>
> Carl Jung, *Memories, Dreams, Reflections*

There are three components to any ethical decision: first, a set of factual circumstances; second, a set of values and principles and thirdly, and most importantly, a person. Although this would seem to be obvious, some rule-oriented ethicists speak as though the facts and the principles alone are all that is needed to form an ethical decision: once these are supplied, the outcome is predestined with robot-like precision. However, this rule-oriented approach destroys our very humanity and individuality. It destroys the individual freedom upon which this nation was founded. And, certainly, to paraphrase Jung, an ethical answer that does not come from within the individual ultimately means very little. The individual must then ultimately create his or her own ethical resolution to any predicament he is facing. Ethical resolutions are therefore inherently unpredictable because of the infinite variations of the interplay between the person, the circumstances and the set of values and principles that may apply to any situation. Let us examine separately each of these components.

## THE PERSON

*In many cases in psychiatry, the patient who comes to us has a story that is not told, and which as a rule no one knows of. To my mind, therapy only really begins after the investigation of that wholly personal story. It is the patient's secret, the rock against which he is shattered. If I know his secret story, I have a key to the treatment.*

Carl Jung, *Memories, Dreams, Reflections*

Part of the beauty and wonder of nature is that we are all significantly and substantially different from one another. At any given point in our lives, we are the product of not only our genetic and physiological heritage, but the upbringing and nurturing by our parents and the people around us. All of us received some blessings and nurturing as children and, unfortunately, many of us received significant psychological and physical wounds as children. It is this combination of nature, nurture and abuse that makes us what we are and ultimately how we perceive the "outside" world to be.

In a mysterious way, we believe what we believe because of the way we were brought up and, in particular, the way we were raised as children. Unfortunately, all of us have been wounded to some degree as children. We may have been wounded by being too smothered or, alternatively, by being not cared for enough. We may have been hurt by being too disciplined or not disciplined enough. We may have been physically and emotionally abandoned as a child or, what may be worse, never allowed to have any privacy, individuality, independence or freedom to think on our own. Since no one's childhood was perfect and no parents are perfect, you need not ask yourself, "Were you wounded as a child?" Instead, simply open your heart and mind and search for the source of your wounds. It will be these wounds that most drastically affect your ethical thinking and that are likely to create extremes in ethical thinking.

If you are among the "flaming liberals:" pro-choice, against the death penalty, and for death with dignity, ask yourself how did you get to be that way? Of course, your views are a product of a lifetime of thinking and reading, but doesn't it also have something to do with maybe rebelling from parents who either smothered you with unhealthy attention and control or, on the other hand, left you totally undisciplined, with no sense of responsibility to yourself, your society or other people?

What if you consider yourself an "arch conservative:" pro-life, pro-death penalty, and against death with dignity or euthanasia statutes? Of course, again, your views are a product of years of thinking and reading, but ask yourself if, somehow or other, your views also have something to do with being emotionally abandoned as a child. Are you in rebellion against the irresponsibility of your parents? Or were you so excessively disciplined and controlled as a child that you cannot allow any freedom in either your life or the lives of others? Perhaps you are not psychologically prepared either to reject everything that your parents taught you or to admit that your parent's love was not completely healthy or mature.

Such psychological wounding can ultimately lead to horrific violence. Consider the murder of Dr. John Britton, killed outside a Florida abortion clinic in 1994. He was killed by shotgun blast to his head by a well known anti-abortion activist, Paul Jennings Hill, age 40. Paul Hill signalled his fanatic pro-life position by declaring after his arrest, "I know one thing: no innocent babies are going to be killed in that clinic today." It comes as no surprise that Paul Hill was pretty much a loser in the rest of his life. He had, prior to the murders, been "self-employed" working on cars in Pensicola. He was a former Presbyterian minister who was ex-communicated in 1993 for his support of the previous murder of an abortion doctor, Dr. Gunn. He was described as both bitter and isolated, even within his fundamentalist Christian church network. A year before the murder, he had written he felt like an outcast for not being able to take the Lord's Supper.[6] I have little doubt that, were we to explore the childhood and early adult life of Paul Hill, we would find the same level of dysfunction and psychological abandonment that exists in the lives of most other killers. However, the isolation, frustration and fanaticism of Paul Hill is just an extreme example of how we are wounded as children and as adults. In differing degrees and at different times in our lives, we have all had to work through the emotional and psychological deficits of our upbringing.

In my own life, I experienced very early an inevitable rebellion against both strict but loving parents and a Southern culture that branded almost everything evil and immoral: sex, abortion, divorce, alcohol and homosexuals. The Southern states have also had no qualms about executing criminals, who, statistically, turned out to be mainly blacks. It has taken some time to shift back from that early rebellion and see that there are some very valid reasons for our society's rules, just as there are at times equally valid reasons for not following rules whenever greater principles must have the final say.

The famous psychoanalyst Carl Jung wrote that the key to understanding the individual was to seek the psychic wound often concealed consciously or unconsciously as a secret by the patient.[7] Similarly, the key to understanding the source of our ethical beliefs may also be to seek our own secret wounds, whether they are the wounds of our childhood or our lives as adults. When we come to understand our own individual wounds, we will be taking a first step toward understanding that our wounds may be different from those of others. We may be taking a first step toward accepting the power and validity of other ethical viewpoints and, ultimately, we may move toward greater understanding of others' most deeply held beliefs. We may come to view our ethical decisions as courses navigated in a sea of ethical principles and realize that the direction taken by one individual may be as ethically valid as that chosen by his neighbor.

## Applying Our Principles To The "Facts"

We all think of a "fact" as something "out there" that cannot be controverted—it either exists or it does not exist. And the statement of its existence is either true or false. However, in ethical decision making, what counts is the perception of the facts, not the facts as they may exist in some scientific reality. Consequently, two people's perception of one identical set of facts and circumstances may give rise to two distinct ethical realities, which must ultimately be honored by our laws and our judicial system.

Consider the famous picture on the next page of the old woman versus the young beauty. Do you see the figure of an old woman, or only the young beauty? Or can you see that both the old woman and the young beauty exist in some sense together within the same drawing? There may be only one drawing, but there are indeed two equally valid perceptions. Applying this understanding to ethical considerations, we must see that, for example, in the case of abortion, two women in identical "external" circumstances may reach opposite ethical decisions on whether to have an abortion. Imagine for instance two teenagers, pregnant as a result of a careless night of drinking. One woman may choose to bring the child to full term, believing that she is capable of either rearing the child or allowing the child to be adopted. The other woman may feel herself totally incapable of coping emotionally with the pregnancy, the child rearing or the prospect of losing the child once born and so perceives the only thing to do is to abort the fetus. The ethical reality is that both of these women can be making moral and ethical decisions. In a very real sense, each of the women's decisions is ethically correct if, in their hearts and after great soul searching, they believe their decision to be the only one they are

morally capable of reaching. In essence, it is the honesty and depth of their ethical search that renders their conflicting decisions both ethically valid.

As another example, consider two cases of criminals convicted of similarly brutal murders. The two juries hearing the two trials may in fact reach two entirely separate results, one imposing the death penalty while the other one does not. In one case, the jury perceives the defendant as a mentally abused individual who will respond in time to intensive psychological and medical rehabilitation. The other jury perceives the defendant, although he committed the same acts, to be a hardened and ruthless criminal with no hope or desire for rehabilitation. Furthermore, as we will address later, that defendant does not request any medical or psychological intervention that would render him harmless to society. In these two separate cases, the imposition of the death penalty in the one case and not in the other does not create an ethical inconsistency, but instead merely reflects two separate ethical realities found within two cases similar only in the "external" facts, that is, the criminal allegations.

The Menendez trial in Los Angeles is an excellent example of the lengths to which the criminal justice system goes to honor the differences between defendants. Although both brothers were accused of murdering their parents in the same shooting, they received different juries because the evidence against them was not absolutely identical. Undoubtedly, the Menendez trial is also a compelling example of the impossibility of trying to pigeonhole a decision about criminal conduct into any rigid set of pre-existing rules. In the first trial, neither jury was able to agree on whether the defendant's admitted killings constituted first degree murder, second degree murder, or voluntary or involuntary manslaughter. I will discuss the evident need for a more flexible conviction and sentencing system in the chapter on criminal law reform.

On the issue of death with dignity, why should we all be circumscribed by one capacity to endure disability and suffering? In two cases of terminally ill patients, both suffering from the same disease and the same amount of pain, why should one person with less capacity to endure pain be considered immoral or unethical because he chooses to terminate his life sooner than another person who is equipped with a different capacity to endure pain? Why do those with a different philosophy of life who choose to continue life until it naturally terminates, regardless of the pain, get to control the lives of others by excluding the option of death with dignity? Indeed, the very essence of a true ethical issue is that individuals may disagree on its resolution in their own lives!

Our ethical principles and legal institutions must avoid ethical absolutism, not only because it precludes recognition of the myriad variations among individuals and individual circumstances, but also because, in the final analysis, there are no "ethical absolutes." The ethical prescription, for example, "Thou shalt not kill," contains virtually no clear directive as to how to handle individual cases and situations. As an example, consider whether it would have been ethical to assassinate Hitler to avoid the horrors of World War II. Since it undoubtedly would have been, clearly there can be no blanket proscription against all killing. Furthermore, in a profound and philosophical sense, such directives do not truly reflect reality because uncertainty is part of all reality, including the reality of both the physical and ethical world.

One of the most compelling and fascinating recent scientific theories in modern physics is applicable to this ethical debate. The Uncertainty Principle formulated in 1926 by Werner Heisenberg sets forth the theory that the actual position and velocity of a subatomic particle could never be precisely determined, because the short wavelength light rays necessary to detect their location would in fact alter the speed of the particle. Thus, it is theoretically impossible to measure accurately both the speed and position of a particle. In short, there is no certain location of ultimate matter! This theory meant the end to a view of science that all the events of the universe were determined and therefore predictable. However, this theory has been generally accepted at this time within the scientific community.[8] Thus, even in the so-called "hard-and-fast" science of physics, there is no "certain physical reality" and there is no "hard material substance" out there to comfort us in our thought that we are living in a "real" and "ordered" world. This experiment might be diagrammed as follows.

LIGHT RAYS ⟶ PARTICLES (Particle, Particle, Particle, Particle)

Just as the particles are affected by the light, and, are, hence, uncertain, so too are our ethical considerations indeterminate. Here is a simplistic representation of what occurs in any ethical decision:

PERSON ⟶ PRINCIPLES ⟶ FACTS (Fact, Fact, Fact, Fact)

Whenever we try to apply ethical principles to see the "facts," our ethical perception actually alters the "facts" just as the light rays alter the particles in the physical experiments. There are, therefore, no certain ethical rules "out there" to be discovered and followed!

The simple truth that must not be overlooked is that it takes a *person* to make an ethical decision and, hence, as each individual determines the facts and ethical principles, their ethical decisions are naturally *unpredictable*. Again, this is because they themselves create the facts and principles as much as they "find" them. As with the picture of the old woman and the young beauty, we create what we see as much as we simply observe it.

It is, of course, surprising to discover that "hard matter" is made up of whirling subatomic particles of unascertainable position and speed. However, in the realm of ethics, we also must realize that there are no clear-cut, hard-and-fast ethical rules that exist for us to follow, if only we could find them! Since each person creates his ethical decisions, inevitably, there are a variety of ethical observations and decisions that may be drawn from any given situation. Accordingly, in the ethical issues that we will examine, let us remember that the institutions and legal principles that we create must allow for this uncertainty and variation. Dramatic differences in both humans and circumstances make it impossible to decide once and for all time that one and only one set of rules for life and death issues can be crowned "ethical."

# Mystery Number 5
# "Evil" Is Dead!

*There is nothing either good or bad,
but thinking makes it so.*

William Shakespeare, *Hamlet*

## The Perils of "Either-or-ism"

The fifth mystery of ethical decision is that its cultural mainstay and its historic key components, Good and Evil, do not really exist! Certainly, they have never existed in the way that trees, pots and pans, or cars exist. They do not even exist in the sense that the scientific law of gravity exists. Instead, as Shakespeare phrased it many centuries ago, they are only creations of our minds. And, hopefully, if we created them, we can also replace them with new concepts.

Unfortunately, however, over the centuries of our ethical and religious development, we have deluded ourselves into thinking that good and evil actually exist somewhere in the material and spiritual world and that people or things are either one or the other. A person is either good or evil. A decision is either good or evil. And in any given case, we can and must choose between good and evil. The terms are, of course, mutually exclusive, so that no person and no ethical decision can escape being ultimately labeled one or the other.

Very few of us fully understand the sweeping and devastating impact this "either/or" mentality has had upon us as individuals and as a nation. This divisive programming was imposed on us all from youth. For many of us as young children, we suffered from the dilemma of deciding whether we had committed an "unforgivable" sin and hence were forever among the "damned" or, what may have been equally bad, we were among the "chosen" ones and therefore separated emotionally from our fellow human beings. This dichotomy reminds me of the bumper sticker "Nice girls go to heaven, bad girls go everywhere!" Certainly, if that were one's only choice, being "bad" would be the best alternative! Fortunately, it is not!

This separatist theology and ethics has been our personal heritage, indelibly imprinted upon our minds and hearts. I remember as a child the intense fear of not knowing whether I had already committed the one "unpardonable sin" and would therefore be condemned to hell! This fear was made all the worse because no one seemed to be able to explain exactly what this one unpardonable sin was! Certainly, it didn't help me to be told finally that the one unpardonable sin was "rejection of the holy spirit." What, pray tell, was that? Perhaps you had a similar childhood wound? Recall how awful it felt to realize that what you had based your entire life on was not "true" after all! Isn't one of our greatest fears to realize that someone else's ethical and religious views are as true and valid as our own?

In my own college years, I remember an evening of loneliness and despair when I suddenly realized all of my strict theological orientation and upbringing was simply unbelievable and, worse, unreasonable and unloving. I walked around the campus for hours, wondering if life was worth living and feeling very much cast adrift, with no clear course of where to go, what to believe, or whether I was, after all, loved. It was a painful rebirth, a shedding of the old ways and a step toward new understanding. It was one of many experiences in my life that terrified me at the time, but which I would not trade for anything.

This theology of "either-or-ism" is still practiced and preached fervently today. Thousands still flock to evangelists to experience religious conversions that once and for all guarantee their acceptance into heaven. They thus may create, however innocently, the divisive distinction that they are "saved" and other people are not! The worst manifestation of this form of salvation becomes "I'm saved...you're not!" Regrettably, this mentality can also extend to "I know what is right...you don't." Unfortunately, when this theology becomes the basis for blanket moral rules such as the condemnation of all abortions, the tragic result is a deep division and hatred within our country. How much more desirable a theology that embraces all people as sons and daughters of God, and that accepts the moral choices of each person as they journey through life!

Whether you have been part of such fundamental faith or not, we have all been indoctrinated into a world of the all-pervasive "either/or." Even if we did not grow up wondering if we were among the "saved" or not, we inevitably grew up in a world of "good guys" versus "bad guys," "cops-versus-robbers," the "enemy" versus "us." We all knew, without question, that the Germans of Nazi Germany were "evil" and that we were "good." We knew that the defeat of Hitler was a moral imperative; and that the Cold War against Communism was our moral and ethical quest, like the Crusades of the twelfth century.

Vietnam was our first dramatic lesson that this simplistic thinking could lead to moral chaos and tragedy. In the beginning, few questioned that we were "good" and the North Vietnamese were "evil." We failed to learn from the French that using force to control the hearts and spirits of another people in another culture half way around the world would result in a tragic waste of life. The casualties of the French armies from 1946 to 1954 were 47,500 killed and 43,000 wounded.[9] Then, from 1954 through 1973, the United States took over the struggle, at an ultimate cost of 58,151 dead and more than 300,000 wounded, plus a financial loss of $165 billion, with nothing to show for all the lives lost but grief and despair.[10] Most people look back upon this war as a great tragedy and mistake, but in the 60's it took both great courage and wisdom to renounce the war. Remarkably, we have now elected a president, Bill Clinton, who avoided the war, and a vice president, Al Gore, who volunteered for the war! And, given the circumstances of their lives at the time, undoubtedly both acted conscientiously and ethically in reaching their decisions.

More recently, in 1991, the world community undertook to resolve the conflict in the Persian Gulf with force, with the result of over 100,000 lives lost and no change in the leadership of Iraq. Certainly, from a moral standpoint, we cannot ethically argue that it was a moral victory because almost all of the men, women and children killed were on the "other side," or that most of those killed were men! The truth is that we have progressed little, if at all, from the "them" versus "us," "either/or" mentality of the Dark Ages!

Let us turn to the world of art to explore visually this divisive heritage. This "either/or" "good versus bad" mentality was graphically illustrated in Michelangelo's famous painting, *The Last Judgment*, completed in 1541. It illustrates the separatist thinking of the sixteenth century. Heaven and hell are clearly demarcated and the people depicted are either saved or condemned. There is nothing in between. You either go down to hell...or up to heaven. So people are either redeemed by God's grace, or they are not. This magnificent painting illustrates how we have come to believe that our ethical decisions are either "right" or "wrong," since people are ultimately either good or bad, saved or damned.

We must escape the treachery of this divisive and destructive mentality, but where can we turn culturally and ethically? We must embrace an ethical philosophy that accepts competing truths taken as a whole. This ethical evolution may be seen in a visual sense, in a revolutionary painting by J.M.W. Turner, who lived from 1775 to 1851. He is regarded as one of the greatest of British artists and probably the greatest landscape painter. His paintings were essentially representational, with clearly demarcated seas, land and sky. But toward the end of his life, his work evolved into dramatic revelations of the wholeness of life, the interdependence and interconnectedness of all of life. Thus, in 1843, Turner painted his visionary *The Morning after the Deluge*, seen on the cover of this book and on page 41.

The painting is a masterpiece of light and color, foreshadowing the Impressionists. But its significance for us is that, for one of the first occasions in history, an artist expressed the ebb and flow of human and divine destiny, with mankind being swirled up into and a part of the more heavenly region where the figure of Moses appears, symbolizing the salvation of all mankind. There is no delineation between heaven and earth, sky and land; instead, all matter and life are part of a whole. Indeed, the entire painting is in the form of a circle, a mandala, which in Indian philosophy represents the unity and oneness of reality.

This beautiful painting reveals an understanding that Turner somehow sensed in 1843 that we in 1995 have yet to grasp: that we are all part of one family on this earth, that to think and believe in terms of black or white, good or bad, us versus them, is to miss both the wonder of God's creation and the woundedness of us all. It is to lose the mystery and purpose of why we are here, alive on the planet Earth.

*Michelangelo,* The Last Judgment. *1534-41*

*J.M.W. Turner,* The Morning after the Deluge. *1843*

## Snow White Without a Witch?

We can certainly forgive ourselves if we are caught up in this either/or mentality, since we were bombarded by it and saturated with it from early childhood. However, escaping the divisive either/or mentality will require us to reject many of the treasured fables and folklore of our culture. Consider, for example, the famous tale of Snow White. Several years ago, I had returned for Thanksgiving vacation with my mother in Tennessee. One evening, my young cousins and I were watching the movie "Snow White" on T.V. I hardly expected that watching this age-old classic would be a decisive point in my thinking about morality and ethics. Yet, suddenly I began to see the film as I had never seen it before. The pure innocence and goodness of the virgin Snow White princess, pitted against the black evil of the witch, struck me in a powerful, religious experience. I realized for the first time a reality that rang unmistakably clear and true: *Snow White needed the witch! There could be no Snow White without the wicked witch! One could not exist without the other!*

I felt like someone who has just realized he has been conned! The revelation brought into question the meaning and validity of all the good guy-bad guy, good-versus-evil, right-versus-wrong fables, stories, religions and wars that made up my culture and hence my very being. I saw the Snow White story for the first time as a travesty and a tragedy, perpetrating the sort of either-or, good-or-evil mentality that has cost untold lives and tragedy throughout history, most notably the loss of 50,000 Americans in Vietnam.

This revelation about Snow White did not, however, imply that force and violence are never justified. We obviously need a police force and the military to protect and defend ourselves, both as individuals and as a nation. However, we must also realize that we *create* our enemies as often as we *find* them. If you doubt this, consider that we are now friends and trade commercially with all of our old enemies: Germany, Japan, Russia and Vietnam! I believe, then, that we must understand that our enemies are not evil creatures just because we are taught to hate them! Nor are they to be punished as we, the arbiters of right and wrong, decide. We would be much better off if we approached other people and nations as simply wanting or not wanting what we want. But we should not label them evil simply because they are different from us or have different goals.

There is, however, some valid use for what might be called the positive aspect of witches, in an archetypal sense. Recently, in my own life, I have come to realize that we are better off accepting the "witch" within us, rather than projecting witches onto other people or peoples, or, worse yet, denying that there are any witches in this sense altogether. This is what I understand Robert Bly to mean when he says we must "swallow our own witch." In his work, *A Little Book on the Human Shadow*, Bly warns against repressing that part of our lives:

> If a boy has given his witch to his mother, and then, when older, has given it to his wife or lover, one day, perhaps at the age of thirty-five or forty, he will feel soft and diminished, precisely because his witch is out there. We can say that the witch corresponds to a force in us that wants to block our growth, yet we must say that the witch presents a very positive force also. Her value lies in the fact that she knows what she wants.[11]

Bly does a marvelous portrayal of the Hansel and Gretel story, in which the witch tries to push the young children into the oven, but gets pushed in herself. I can still hear his voice crackling as he imitated the witch! What I learned from him is simply that witches have at least one saving grace: they know exactly what they want! I understand that I, for one, would be better off imitating them in that way, rather than wasting my life trying to decide what other people felt I should do with my life, or sitting around complaining about the misdeeds of other people! In terms of the Snow White saga, she really didn't need a witch to make her life meaningful and exciting. Nor do we, as a nation, need external enemies to make our American experience challenging and rewarding. What we do need is to tackle the toughest challenge that any of us face: decide what we really want in our lives...and do it!

## THE SEARCH FOR EVIL

*Don't ask for the meaning...ask for the use.*

Ludvig Wittgenstein, author of
*Philosophical Investigations*

Clearly, the downside of the evil versus good mentality is evil itself. We do not need to worry about good, but evil obviously brings with it hurt, pain and separation. We all find ourselves wondering about evil—whether it exists and where it comes from. Is there any other way to explain the horrors of life and our inhumanity to each other? For some people, the question becomes one of life-and-death critical importance. A turning point in my own father's life occurred when he asked his minister, "Will evil always be with us?" Unfortunately, the answer to this type of question always depends on who you ask! Our minister was a Presbyterian, raised and educated within a theology of predestination, without question the zenith of either-or-ism! Predestination says that you are predestined to be saved or not, even before birth! In fact, there is no way to be absolutely sure if you are among the saved or not, although good works may at least give you some psychological relief. In more personal terms, you were either good and went to heaven or evil and went to hell! Our minister's inevitable reply was, therefore, "Yes." From that point on, my father seemed to lose hope in life and ultimately fell into greater and greater despair.

I have inherited this same burning interest in the ethics and theology of evil from my father. Hopefully, and by grace, I have resolved it in a manner that has given me a much more promising understanding of what human nature is all about. Let me share with you this understanding by taking you with me on an ethical/visual journey.

Are you ready to go? All you will need to bring on this journey will be your honesty and memory. This will be a visual adventure and I suggest that you prepare for it by finding a quiet place where you will not be interrupted. Now, let's sit down and start off with a few deep relaxing breaths of air.

## A Guided Ethical Mediation

Begin to recall into your memory all those people, men and women, whom you have met or come to know and who you can say you fully understand. These will be people whom, through the years, you have come to understand so well that you know them almost as well as you know yourself. These people who you will call before you, to stand before you in your mind's eye, may be friends, family, lovers, partners, enemies, clients—in fact, any one of whom you can say, "I fully understand them." You would probably have to know a lot about their childhood and know how they grew up to become the way they are. You would have had to walk with them and talk with them for some time to fully know them. Take as much time as you need to do this visual exercise. If there is any question in your mind whether you know what makes a person "tick" or why they behave the way they do, then leave them out of this gathering group of men and women standing before you in your mind's eye. Remember, these are not people who you necessarily like or admire. They may be people that you truly find abhorrent, but do not allow them to stand in front of you unless you can say, "I know them as well as I know myself."

Now ask yourself one simple question: is any one of these men or women evil? That is, can you honestly and truly say to yourself that any one of the people that you know this well are people that you feel are inherently and without question evil?

◆

If your answer is no, then you are certainly in good company, for in the numerous times that I have posed this question and presented this guided exercise to various men's groups and religious groups, the answer uniformly has always been the same. Only an occasional person has raised his hand or stood up when asked if any of the people that they fully understood was evil. When I present this visual exercise, I ask everyone to open their eyes and look around the room to see if anyone is raising his hand or standing up in the affirmative. It is awe inspiring to see that virtually no one, in their personal experience, thinks there are truly evil people! In the cases where one or two people have raised their hands, they have usually described a person unknown to them except for a great harm or crime they caused someone else. I asked the people gathered there to take note of this and accept what blessing this may be to their own understanding.

This very simple exercise establishes why the concept of evil is really of no value in ethical thinking. The truth is that when we fully understand people, we never consider them evil. If we follow Wittgenstein's advice to seek the use of a word, not its meaning, we discover that evil is just the word we use to describe people who are distant to us and who have or will hurt us. Thus, foreigners or people distant to us or people we do not truly know get labeled "evil" as a scapegoat method of taking usually drastic disciplinary, punitive or warlike measures against them. Thus, Saddam Hussein is labeled evil to justify our bombing and killing of hundreds of thousands of people in the Middle East. Criminals who commit horrific crimes are labeled evil as opposed to sick, to justify the imposition of the death penalty.

In short, anyone with whom we violently disagree and whose conduct we are willing to use drastic measures to change may be called evil. But since it is clear that we never use the word evil in conjunction with those people we truly understand, maybe it is time that we as a people and as a nation stop using the word altogether.

To paraphrase the sharing of an elder at one of my men's renewal weekends, any one of us, nurtured in an atmosphere of love and caring, will grow up to be a person who can love and be at peace with himself. But cursed by abusive and demented parents, almost every one of us would grow up criminals.

In our everyday speech, the opposite of love is usually said to be evil or hate. Love and hate are either/or dualisms, just like good versus evil. I have come to believe, however, that we as a nation would be much better off to dismiss this dualistic thinking from our vocabularies, minds and spirits. In short, I propose that we think of love or goodness much as we do gravity; there is no opposite of gravity; that is, things have more or less gravity, but there is no theory or force that exists in opposition to gravity. More simply put, "gravity" has no opposite. Similarly, I believe we should think of people as more or less loving or good, not evil versus good. What we call evil then is really just another name for unloved. Pure evil, then, is really the complete absence of love or good. I believe that this change in thinking will lead to greater happiness in our homes, cities and within our nation. Of course, ceasing to use the word "evil" will not by itself put an end to crime, suffering and hurt. But it should lead us to more compassionate and enlightened thinking, just as ceasing to use such derogatory words as "nigger," "spic" and "faggot" leads to a more loving, tolerant society.

Here is another analogy: when you go to bed at night, you don't say to your spouse, "Please turn on the darkness," (unless of course, you are really weird)! Instead, you say, "Please turn out the light." This is simply because we know, and our language reflects, that while light rays actually exist, darkness is merely the absence of light. Darkness really means "absence of light;"

it does not refer to something that exists on its own. And we know that the way to "combat" darkness is not to try to "attack" it, because it doesn't exist; we solve darkness by providing light. In the same way, we must fight "evil" simply by promoting good. Unfortunately, for centuries we have been trying to fight something (evil) that does not exist!

As Christ said, "Let he who is without evil cast the first stone." We *all* have the capacity for good and evil. Any child subjected to cruel abuse can become a criminal. A child nurtured in love will invariably grow up to be happy and productive. If this is true, why should we label anyone evil? To label anyone evil is to strip away their very humanity and dignity. We must finally realize we should not label anyone evil anymore than it is loving or right to call someone a queer or a witch. Furthermore, our choice of words is important: words manifest our true feelings and mold our actions. Once we have labeled someone evil, we can do just about anything we want to that person and be justified.

For centuries, we have been seduced by the concept of good versus evil, with other people or peoples always being the evil ones. Hopefully, in the near future, the concept of good versus evil will inevitably take its place in history along with such cultural myths as slavery, predestination and witchcraft! It will be replaced by a more basic understanding of the value and meaning of life, such as the concept of the capacity to love and be loved. Fortunately, although the concept of good versus evil has existed since the beginning of mankind, we are already seeing cracks in the fortress wall of this antiquated and repressive approach to human existence.

## The "Blame Game" Is Over

Ethical and moral breakthroughs do in fact occur, and we as a society have evolved to higher ethical plains. For example, in the United States barely one hundred years ago, many still felt that slavery was moral and legal and that women, by virtue of their inferiority, were inherently incapable of voting! As Albert Einstein said, "Excellent ideas have always encountered violent opposition from mediocre minds." So, I am convinced that the concept of evil will be looked upon one hundred years from now with the same incredulous disbelief that we now hold for the concept of God as a white-haired father figure high in the sky, along with the belief that the earth is flat!

In recent political debates, the clash between these world views has been seen in a more dramatic fashion. Some candidates point out the critical need for elected officials who can make decisions, arguing that you "can't have it both ways" and you cannot "waffle" on issues. You must side for or against abortion, and be for or against the death penalty. Wiser candidates, however, reflect a truer sense of evolved ethical thinking by arguing against the all-or-nothing, either/or mentality: their vision is that the best of worlds is often a position in between two warring schools of thought.

Signs of the evolution towards a more unified and holistic ethical thinking are readily apparent. As a practicing lawyer in the California court system, I am frequently surprised when clients come to me for a divorce and are not aware, at least not fully and emotionally aware, that the court system has absolutely no interest whatsoever in the cause of the divorce or for determining who was "at fault." California's no-fault divorce statute has been in effect since 1970. Unfortunately, in states such as New York, the fault principle was in effect until 1967, forcing parties to have to make up a "wrong," such as infidelity, in order to be granted a divorce! Often, most divorcing couples would flip a coin to see who would be the "bad guy." Little wonder that the public often has no respect for the absurdities of the law!

I know of no practicing attorney or anyone involved in the divorce court system who wishes that we could return to the fault system of the past. The divorce system as it stands is sufficiently fraught with delay, emotional grief and costs in dividing up property and awarding support on a neutral basis. Furthermore, in the area of child custody, there is likewise no consideration of who was at fault in the divorce or even who is the "best" person. Instead, custody is awarded in the best interest of the children, regardless of the cause of the divorce or the rightness or wrongness of people's positions.

Similar inroads into the fault system are occurring in other areas of the law. In many states, including California, medical malpractice actions have been severely and rigidly limited, so that regardless of the degree of the physician's fault or state of the plaintiff's disfigurement, disability or pain and suffering, the maximum award that a person can receive for pain and suffering is $250,000. By comparison, the maximum in the state of Maryland is $350,000. One net result of this is that if you become a quadriplegic from a vehicle accident in California, you can receive many millions of dollars for your injuries, but if you become a quadriplegic as a result of a physician's negligence, the most you can receive for pain and suffering is $250,000. Obviously, the disparities created within the tort system by this inequality are wrong. Arguably, in the medical malpractice arena, the value of such limitations is that it puts a cap on the liability of physicians and thereby lowers insurance premiums, supposedly affording lower cost medical care to all people. However, for our focus, the limits on medical malpractice awards only demonstrate another area in which court awards based on fault and negligence are being severely curtailed.

Another dramatic example of the curtailment of the fault system are the limitations now placed on the death penalty. The death penalty was originally struck down by the landmark 1972 Supreme Court case of *Furman v. Georgia*.[12] In that case, two of the petitioners were convicted of rape in Georgia and were sentenced to death. Both felons were black and both victims were white. The court held that the death penalty constituted cruel and unusual punishment because it was imposed in an arbitrary manner without effective guidelines. Justice Stewart emphasized its random imposition.

> These death sentences are cruel and unusual in the same way that being struck by lightning is cruel and unusual. For, of all the people convicted of rapes and murders in 1967 and 1968, many just as reprehensible as these, the petitioners are among a capriciously selected random handful upon whom the sentence of death has in fact been imposed...I simply conclude that the Eighth and Fourteenth Amendments cannot tolerate the infliction of a sentence of death under legal systems that permit this unique penalty to be so wantonly and so freakishly imposed.

Thereafter, as a result of tremendous political upheaval, various statutes were adopted that tried to remedy the defect of the criminal death penalty statutes at the time, namely, the lack of any guidelines to avoid random and unequal imposition of the death penalty.

Only four years later, in 1976, the Supreme Court decided *Gregg v. Georgia*,[13] upholding as constitutional a death penalty statute that provided clear guidelines for juries to follow in the imposition of the death penalty. Under the new Georgia system, after the conviction, the jury separately considers whether mitigating circumstances would warrant a lesser sentence than the death penalty. The result is that, the death penalty, once declared unconstitutional as cruel and unusual, regardless of the fault, or evilness of the offense, is now allowed, provided that the jury or judge consider all mitigating circumstances and follow the guidelines justifying the imposition of the ultimate sanction. In the chapter specifically addressing the death penalty, we will look at why such guidelines do make ethical sense and we will also explore a proposal to resolve the controversy surrounding the death penalty.

## The Resurrection Of The Blame Game

Despite the movement away from fault-finding and labeling people or acts as evil, there have been powerful arguments recently advanced to resurrect the concept of evil as a basis for decision making. Most notably in the international arena, there has been the description of Saddam Hussein as an evil person. President Bush consistently described Hussein as a ruthless and evil dictator, thereby justifying the 1991 Persian Gulf war, in which it is estimated that more than 100,000 men were killed in the name of international justice. More recently, President Clinton directed an attack using 23 missiles against an intelligence installation in Baghdad on the grounds that Saddam Hussein's government had authorized an assassination plot against George Bush when he visited Kuwait as a private citizen. This act of retaliation caused the deaths of at least eight civilians and numerous wounded. Yet we are told that no attempt on our part was made to assassinate Saddam Hussein, since we subscribe to the United Nations agreement prohibiting the assassination of the leader of another country.

I can only wonder in amazement at the ethical logic that results in the deaths of eight innocent civilians, when the most appropriate action against a ruthless dictator would, I believe, be the assassination of that dictator. Our antiquated ethical stand on the issue of assassination reminds me of the old-fashioned way of making war, where both sides lined up in the manly way to shoot at each other, since breaking ranks was cowardly and undignified! Nevertheless, it is certainly beyond the scope of this book and my expertise to argue international politics and warfare. I am simply pointing out that labeling Saddam Hussein or anyone else evil does not necessarily justify any particular corrective action toward that person, nor does it tell us what that action should be. We would be much better off if we simply admitted that, in the case of Saddam Hussein, he was doing things that we felt must be stopped, namely, limiting our access to oil! Adding onto our analysis that he is evil does not by itself give us the right to kill innocent and uninvolved civilians, or 100,000 soldiers. One of the reasons given for our united attack on Iraq was that Saddam Hussein's forces were raping hundreds of innocent Kuwait women. On that basis, however, the United States Armed Forces should invade and occupy the United States, since in 1992, 39,100 American men were arrested for forcible rape. There were also 22,510 arrests for murder, and a total of 14,075,100 arrests for all crimes.[14] We need to address the crimes within our own country before claiming to become the policeman of the world! I believe that the streets of our most crime-ridden areas should be constantly patrolled by our armed forces. Perhaps it is time for us to realize that, just as Luke Skywalker discovered that Darth Vader was his father, we have "met the enemy and the enemy is us!"

Another notable recent effort to resurrect evil as a valid ethical concept has come in the form of a well-respected and noted author, Dr. Scott Peck. In his recent book, *People of the Lie*, Dr. Peck somewhat reluctantly and with great reservation concludes that evil exists, that it is a disease and that it can be treated. After explaining how he came to believe in the evil of some of his patients, Dr. Peck rediscovers evil as a "distinct new type of personality disorder." He summarizes the characteristics of such a disorder as follows:

(a) Consistent destructive, scapegoating behavior, which may often be quite subtle.

(b) Excessive, albeit usually covert, intolerance to criticism and other forms of narcissistic injury.

(c) Pronounced concern with a public image and self-image of respectability, contributing to a stability of life-style but also to pretentiousness and denial of hateful feelings or vengeful motives.

(d) Intellectual deviousness, with an increased likelihood of a mild schizophreniclike disturbance of thinking at times of stress.[15]

In the end, however, he classifies evil people as a "variant of the narcissistic personality disorder"![16] This is quite remarkable, since I would have supposed that being labeled evil would be the most inclusive and devastating disorder imaginable! Dr. Peck is clearly defining "evil" in an unusual way, since labeling a person evil has traditionally entitled society to execute such people for their crimes. Instead, under Peck's definition, the essence of evil would include "intolerance to criticism and pronounced concern with public image." Although I am neither a trained psychologist nor a psychiatrist, I can see nothing to be gained by labeling people or peoples evil, especially when our conduct is largely a part of predetermined factors, as Dr. Peck readily admits:

> An individual's evil can almost always be traced to some extent to his or her childhood circumstances, the sins of the parents and the nature of their heredity. Yet evil is always also a choice one has made—indeed a whole series of choices.[17]

Certainly, if we must have a theory of evil, it should be as Dr. Peck proposes—a disease that is to be treated with compassion. However, the down side of continuing to use the word "evil" is that it typically is associated with deliberate and intentional criminal and illegal conduct, which justifies the imposition of the most severe sanctions up to the death penalty. It is, therefore, a theoretical mechanism by which we can separate ourselves from others, condemning them as unfit to live. If our societal and international goal is to promote harmony, peace and prosperity among all peoples, I can see no purpose served by promoting a concept that has at its core meaning the division of human beings one from the other.

Just what did Dr. Peck gain by reinventing a theory of evil to treat his patients? For example, Dr. Peck writes that he wished that he diagnosed patient "Charlene" as being evil early on in his treatment. This was for various reasons: she seemed to be playing with him and not sincerely interested in progressing in her many years of treatment. He writes that the most significant cause of her failure to be psychologically healed was her failure to regress to a childhood state, through which he could treat and diagnose her childhood wounds. Ultimately, she was labeled evil by her therapist:

> Be that as it may, there were many times when Charlene seemed to be moved by desires beyond my comprehension—motives so obscure as to be out of the range of my human experience. More than anything else, it is this "inhuman" something, out of reach of ordinary psychodynamic understanding, that I have labeled—rightly or wrongly—evil. But I cannot be absolutely certain whether it was alien to me because it was evil or whether I called it evil because it was so alien.[18]

In another case, the parents of "Roger" were labeled evil because they, too, were playing games with Dr. Peck and were not truly interested in helping their depressed son. Specifically, they did not agree with Dr. Peck that their son should be sent to boarding school! It is tempting to suggest, tongue-in-cheek, that one definition of Dr. Peck's concept of evil is "not immediately agreeing with Dr. Peck"! I say tongue-in-cheek because I do not doubt for one moment the sincerity, love and care of Dr. Peck for his patients. However, I do strongly disagree with Dr. Peck that either individuals or our society as a whole can profit from dredging up the concept of evil as a basis for how we treat or judge other people. Instead, I propose that we start thinking about people as being more or less loving, more or less mentally healthy or more or less good, not good versus evil.

There is nothing at all new, by the way, about this proposal. As long ago as the Fifth Century B.C., Plato argued that no one actually wants to be evil or do evil acts. Instead, people do wrongful or hurtful acts due to their own ignorance or lack of knowledge. Evil, then, results from failure to understand what is good. People will naturally do what is good and what is best for them and best for the people as a whole, if they have a loving upbringing and are educated about ethical truths. There is even an "honor among thieves" that makes it possible for them to conduct their business with efficiency and for the good of their limited group. In *The Republic,* he wrote the following:

> Now when we say that the just are shown to be wiser and better and more able to act effectively, and the unjust to be incapable of accomplishing anything together, and when on the other hand we add that in fact those who do accomplish something with strong united action are yet sometimes unjust people—then we are not saying what is wholly true; for they could not have kept their hands off each other if they were absolutely unjust; it is clear that some justice was in them, which kept them from wronging each other as well as those they attacked, and by this justice they accomplished as much as they did. They set out on their unjust way only demidevils in wickedness, since whole villains, and men perfectly unjust, are perfectly unable to act effectively.[19]

Thus, by arguing that evil is essentially the absence of good, I am merely asking us to revisit the wisdom of Plato and start treating each other as inherently good, provided we are loved, trained and nurtured as children, not hated and abandoned.

## THE WISDOM OF OLD AGE

America is now over two centuries old. Certainly we are in what might be called the mid-life of our country. It is time then, that our ethics, laws and judicial institutions reflect the wisdom and maturity that come with age. One of the hallmarks of such maturity is the ability to tolerate and understand both other people and other people's ethical viewpoints, even when they directly conflict with our own. Just as individuals must, if they are to progress, become more tolerant and understanding as they age, so must our nation develop such understanding as well.

The ethical progression and maturation of people in mid-life has been excellently described by Dr. Allan B. Chinen in his delightful book, *Once Upon a Midlife*. Dr. Chinen uses mythic tales that illuminate what happens or should happen as we reach middle age. In the discussion on "The Challenge of Evil," he tells the story of a shopkeeper whose life was saved because he followed the advice of a wise man not to meddle in other people's affairs:

> Shortly thereafter, the shopkeeper, returning home through a wilderness, came to a lonely cottage and received shelter from a strange man. After the two had dined, the man opened a door to the cellar and a blind woman came out. The man picked up a human skull, filled it with soup and gave the woman a reed to use as a spoon. When the poor woman finished he locked her back in the cellar.
> 
> "Well, friend," the man asked the shopkeeper, "what do you make of that?" The shopkeeper remembered Solomon's second counsel, *don't meddle in other people's affairs.* So the merchant said "You must have reasons for what you do."

The man of the house smiled grimly, "I do. That witch is my wife. She took another man as her lover but I caught them and killed the man. His skull is the bowl she eats from and her spoon is the reed I used to gouge her eyes out." The merchant felt sickened. "And what do you think of that, friend?" the vengeful husband asked.

The merchant swallowed hard. "If you think you are right, you must be," the shopkeeper said aloud.

"Good," the murderer replied. "Anyone who says I am wrong dies."[20]

Although I am quoting only a small portion of this tale, it symbolically demonstrates the more mature confrontation of evil and tragedy. Clearly, in the tale, the acceptance of another person's viewpoint has saved the life of the character; whereas a younger, more idealistic hero might have drawn his sword and sought to impose his own version of justice upon the man. In this tale, the middle-aged merchant relates to the man and accepts him as he is, as Dr. Chinen explains:

> By midlife most individuals recognize that their moral judgments can be wrong and that other people have different ethical principles. Men and women develop greater tolerance for moral ambiguities and accept that there is no one right answer to any ethical problem. They arrive at a pluralistic attitude toward good and evil. Contrary to stereotypes, individuals usually become more tolerant and less moralistic with age. Younger adults are often morally rigid, because of their uncompromising idealism.[21]

America, too, is at a midlife crossroad in its ethical revolution. We are called upon at this stage in our history to have the greater maturity of the wise person who can see, understand and tolerate opposing ethical views, and to allow people to conduct themselves as their consciences and understanding dictate. Indeed, we have no alternative but to reach such maturity, because, like the merchant in the tale, if we can not tolerate each other, we may end up destroying each other.

# Mystery Number 6

## Identical Acts Of Force May Be Ethical Or Unethical

*Force, and Fraud, are in war the two cardinal virtues.*

Thomas Hobbes, *Leviathan*

*It is the last territorial claim which I have to make in Europe.*

Adolf Hitler, speech, September 26, 1938

1994 marked the 50th anniversary of the Allied Forces' invasion on D-Day on the Normandy coast of France. It was the greatest military amphibious landing in the history of the world and without much dispute, a heroic triumph of good over evil, in antiquated language, or good over the mental illness of a madman, as I would prefer to describe it. This unparalleled use of force ultimately led to the freeing of millions of captured people and the rescue of millions of people from imminent destruction by the Nazis. We have celebrated this anniversary with great reverence and admiration for the men and women who sacrificed their lives for a noble and ethical cause. These forces brought about both the liberation of Europe and the salvation of millions of Jews fated for destruction.

It is unlikely, however, that we will have any such commemorations on the 50th anniversary of the Vietnam war. Although massive forces were similarly used in the name of liberating and protecting a certain group of people, most writers would concede that the more than 50,000 American lives lost in this struggle were given in vain and that no ethical or worthwhile purpose was accomplished by over a decade of military conflict.

What was the difference? Similar amounts of force were involved. I doubt that the easy answer to this difference is that we won World War II and lost the Vietnam war. If, for example, at a cost of an additional 25,000 American lives and 100,000 Vietnamese lives, we could have developed military control of Vietnam, would life in the entire country of Vietnam be any different today? Probably not. In fact, we have just developed trade relations with Vietnam. Yet, in contrast, we think that life in Europe is substantially different today as a result of the outcome of World War II.

Contrasting these two military conflicts serves to illustrate the ethical mystery that identical acts of force may be considered ethical or unethical. Let us consider why this is so and why force in infinitely varying degrees is always a part of ethical decision making.

What comes to your mind when you hear or read the word "force?" Do you think of the kind of force used to drive a nail into wood to construct a home? Or do you think of oppression or brutality by men over innocent and helpless women or helpless people? If your reaction is the latter, please keep in mind that force is an entirely neutral word and that force can be used either for good or not. (I almost said "or evil!")

Recently, when preparing a presentation of the "Mystery of Ethical Decision" with two women members of my church, I was strongly urged by both of them not to include in my talk the use of the word force or any theory relating to force. They felt, probably correctly, that any use of the word force would be misunderstood by some members of the congregation, no matter how carefully I tried to explain, describe or limit it. Specifically, they were afraid some women in the congregation would equate "force" with male domination. However, in this book and in my discussion with you, it is possible to describe precisely what is meant by force and what is not meant by force. And since force is an inevitable part of life, not to mention ethical choices and principles, we must talk about it if we are to have a theory of ethics that is relevant to the real world.

Force is a common part of our everyday lives. In its broadest sense, force is used in everything from breathing in and out to opening and closing doors. *Webster's* defines force as follows.

FORCE.
1. The exertion of physical strength (we had to use force to restrain him) physical vigor, (the force of manhood) mental or moral strength, especially in the overcoming of opposition, by force of argument.[22]

It should come as no surprise that the definition of force includes moral strength, as we have already found that the use of force is an inevitable part of both ethical decision making and ethical principles. By comparison, we normally use the word "violence" to describe conduct that is not ethically justified. *Webster's* describes violence as follows:

VIOLENCE.
1. A use of physical force so as to damage or injure. Intense natural force or energy. An abusive use of force, passion, fury, distortion of meaning. Desecration.
2. To offend, outrage. To do violence to someone else's sense of justice.[23]

If force as defined is an inevitable part of our everyday lives, it must likewise be an inevitable part of the ethical decisions that we make in our everyday lives. Our ethical options are when to use force and how much force to use, not to avoid using force at all. Only a Tibetan monk living in isolation in a mountain hut might approach an ideal of a totally "unforceful" life. However, such a life we can easily dismiss as irrelevant to Americans in this century. Accordingly, as we concentrate on each of our three main areas of ethical concern, we will see that the use of force plays a fundamental role in the ethical questions concerning abortion, criminal justice and death with dignity.

Unfortunately, our American idealism leads us, if anything, too readily into the use of brutal force. The tragedy of the attack on the religious fanatic David Koresh and his followers at Waco, Texas, is a recent example. In the first assault on the compound, four Alcohol, Tobacco and Firearms agents were killed by Koresh's followers. Motivated by a sense of urgency from reports of child abuse, the federal authorities launched a second attack on Koresh's compound, which only played into his demented scheme of Armageddon. Instead of rescuing the innocent children, the result was that the compound was burned and 80 men, women and children died in the flames. This is an example of why I believe that our new national motto on force should be: when in doubt, don't use it! Apparently, the jury in the murder trials of the eleven compound members also reached the same conclusion: all eleven of the Branch Davidians were acquitted of murder, although seven were convicted on lesser charges.[24]

The problem of force v. violence in ethical decision making is that, in any given situation, too little force may be as bad as too much. Of course, it is easy to identify after the fact when too little or too much has been used. And probably everyone has witnessed or suffered a punishment that was as wrong as the crime itself. Consider the experience shared by one of my friends at a men's wisdom counsel.

## STRUCK DOWN BY LOVE?

When it came his turn to speak, my friend David related that he was the son of a tough and "by-the-book" Navy pilot. Once when he was a young teenager, he had struck his younger sister. When his father came home, he confronted David and asked if he had done this. David honestly replied, "Yes, I did." Without warning, the father, a large and powerful man, knocked his son to the ground, bellowing, "Now you know how it feels to be hit by someone larger than you!"

Silence overcame the men in the gathering, as we sensed the inherent tragedy of the situation. David continued, "Although I realized what I had done to my sister was wrong, I sensed at the same time that what my father had done to me was also wrong." The truth of David's words was unmistakable. His wrong as a young boy did not justify or make right the brutal action of his father. In fact, the action of his father in striking him actually taught the wrong lesson: violence inherently always justifies more violence. Miraculously, David realized that what he had done and that what his father had done were both wrong...even as a young boy.

David's story reveals that such use of violence and force is not only unjustified, but it is immoral. It shows that our fierce instinct for release of anger and revenge can overcome our instinct to be loving and caring.

Have you ever been intimidated by a bully? Did resorting to violence help you protect yourself? In the intriguing movie, *Witness*, directed by Peter Weir, Harrison Ford plays a tough Philadelphia cop who has uncovered corruption in the police department. The "bad guy" cops are of course out to kill him, so Ford joins a gentle Amish farming community to escape detection. One day he travels with his Amish friends to town, where the "local yocals" taunt his friends, sticking an ice cream cone on the nose of one of the young men, to see if they could be provoked to fight. Predictably, they honor their religious beliefs and refuse to fight. Still spoiling for a fight, the tough guys next target Harrison Ford. Although in Amish garb, Ford gives one warning, "I wouldn't do that if I were you." Nevertheless, the local hoodlum goes ahead and smears ice cream on Ford's nose as well.

At that point, every red-blooded American cell in my body was crying out, "Teach him a lesson," which, of course, in spectacular box office appeal, Ford does: he breaks the guy's nose with one punch, all to the audience's huge sigh of relief! Yet, that very act revealed Ford's presence in the town and led to his being tracked by his foes.

This is a lesson America never seems to learn—that our brutal use of superior force almost never seems to fulfill our goals, certainly not in the last fifty years. Indeed, our fierce instinct to be a "tough guy" and "just" almost always seems to interfere with our goals. Before we embark on another military crusade, we should read the words of Mark Twain in *The Mysterious Stranger*.

> There has never been a just one, never an honorable one, on the part of the instigator of the war. I can see a million years ahead, and this rule will never change in so many as half a dozen. The loud little handful, as usual, will shout for the war. The pulpit will, warily and cautiously, object at first; the great, big, dull bulk of the nation will rub its sleepy eyes and try to make out why there should be a war and will say, earnestly and indignantly, it is unjust and dishonorable and there is no necessity for it. Then the handful will shout louder. A few fair men on the other side will argue and reason against the war with speech in hand and at first will get a hearing and be applauded, but it will not last long. Those others will outshout them, and presently the anti-war audiences will thin out and lose popularity. Before long you will see this curious thing—speakers stoned from the platform and free speech strangled by hordes of furious men who, in their secret hearts, are still at one with those stoned speakers

as earlier, but do not dare to say so. And now the whole nation, pulpit and all, will take up the war cry, shout itself hoarse, and mob any honest man who ventures to open his mouth. Presently, such mouths will cease to open. Next, the state will invent cheap lies, putting the blame upon the nation that is attacked, and every man will be glad of those conscience-soothing vanities and will diligently study them and refuse to examine any refutation of them, and thus he will, by and by, convince himself that the war is just and will thank God for the better sleep he enjoys after this process of grotesque self-deception.

Although it is easy to tell when too much force has been applied, when we approach brand-new situations, the question is not so easily resolved. This reality has been dramatically revealed every time I have led a workshop discussion using a hypothetical life-and-death situation, which I have entitled "Shipwrecked."

Do you have any friends who feel that force should never be used, no matter what the reason? Or, conversely, that it can always be justified? While driving on a camping trip with my friend Allen, we found ourselves debating the issue of pacifism. I argued the case for a just use of force: "What if we had just been shipwrecked and landed on an island where we immediately encountered a kill-or-be-killed situation?" Allen felt deadly force was never justified. I thought it could be. This debate became the format for a workshop months later at the Unitarian Universalist Men's Fellowship. The task was to resolve in forty-five minutes the following dilemma.

## SHIPWRECKED

You and your two companions, one woman and one man, are the sole survivors of a vessel that sank hundreds of miles from any shipping lanes. In your raft there are provisions for two days of food, a loaded pistol with six bullets, a knife and some first aid equipment. After four exhausting days at sea, your raft beaches on a small island that is not even charted.

It is nearly sunrise as the three of you struggle to shore. Your two friends collapse from fatigue, but you explore the island to find food and water. As you reach the top of a hill, you discover, to your horror, that the island is inhabited by two men and one woman who have imprisoned five people in a corral made of branches. The prisoners are guarded by one man with a rifle, but as the sun rises, the other man and the woman come out from a hut and drag one of the women prisoners into the hut, and, from the sounds that you hear, appear to viciously attack and rape her. Later, the other prisoners are escorted in chains to work in fields as slaves. It is clear to you by the way they beat the prisoners that these three are vicious and sadistic criminals.

As you run back to your companions, you realize in terror that the island is so small that soon you will be discovered by the other three, all of whom have guns. You must take action immediately!

What will you and your friends do?

♦

Our group then divided into three smaller groups to come to grips with this make-believe dilemma. Later, each group returned to the larger group to report on what had been decided. As you might well imagine, the resolutions that were reached ranged from a clear-cut definitive plan of action to no unified plan at all. (This was not surprising, especially if you know anything about Unitarians!) To understand the process of each group, observers had been secretly planted and requested to report later to the group as a whole. They reported three very different approaches to problem solving, ranging from a virtual free-for-all, with no structure or leadership, to a very tightly organized discussion led primarily by one individual.

The observers had been asked to note to what extent force came into play in the reaching of the resolution and decision by the group within the limited time frame. The results are summarized below:

|  | Extent Of Force In Decision Making | Result |
|---|---|---|
| Group 1. | One leader guided voting among succeeding alternatives. | One plan of action to use whatever force is needed to save the victims. |
| Group 2. | Two leaders led the group to a strategy acceptable to all except for the final use of force. | One plan of action with two options of force, one deadly, the other not deadly. |
| Group 3. | No leaders or forcefulness—all contributed equally. | Three plans of action, i.e., no agreement at all on the use of force. |

We may learn two lessons from these workshops. First, in serious life-or-death situations, not only may force be ethically used, it usually must be used. Furthermore, the extent of force required varies with the danger and risk involved. However, both the individual and the social goal is undoubtedly to use the minimum amount of force necessary to achieve a desired outcome.

Secondly, some force or forcefulness is necessary to arrive at an ethical decision. The group that had no leadership or forcefulness to their debate wound up with three plans of action, i.e., in reality, no decision or agreement at all. These people would have perished or become enslaved on the hypothetical island! The groups where leadership was displayed had clear plans of action.

A recent example of the need for force in ethical decision making was found in the jury deliberations of the second trial of the four Los Angeles police officers accused of beating Rodney King. According to some of the jury members, the jury was making no substantial progress in their debate until, at one point, the people's deepest feelings were touched, and anger was expressed openly, to the point that some of the jury members became emotionally disturbed by the violence of the interaction. In fact, one jury member became ill as a result of the clash of wills and view points. However, it was only after that venting of deep feeling and moral commitment that the jury was able to reach consensus on the terribly difficult issues facing them. They were therefore able to reach definitive verdicts, finding two of the accused guilty and two not guilty of violating Rodney King's constitutional rights. The previous state trial ended in acquittal of the four officers on all but one count, leading to a Los Angeles riot that left fifty-two dead. We see then, that degrees of force are inherent not only in ethical decision making, that is, the process of reaching an ethical decision, but also that force inevitably plays a part in all ethical principles.

I thus would take exception to the pacifist concept that if your enemy strikes you on the left cheek, you should present to him the right as well, since this will only work if you have an enemy whose sense of compassion and caring is sufficiently developed that such nonviolent opposition would make any difference in the first place. For example, Mahatma Ghandhi's campaign of nonviolence worked only because the British public manifested outrage over the brutal treatment of the Indian people by the occupying British forces. He was thus able to secure Indian Independence in 1949 with a minimum of bloodshed. Unfortunately, there was no such sense of compassion among the

Hindus, Muslims, and Sikhs to prevent the bloodbath that followed their independence.

As we approach our three ethical issues, we will rely upon these basic principles: first, force is an inevitable part of both ethical decision making and ethical principles; second, the amount of force, violence or punishment that may ethically be imposed depends on the danger or harm that will result if such action is not taken. For example, what harm will result to the future child and mother if the forceful act of abortion is not performed? What possible harm to other individuals may occur if the criminal career of a vicious murderer is not terminated in one form or other? And finally, what suffering may occur if an individual is not allowed to choose the ultimately forceful act of ending a terminal illness through a dignified death?

## WHY PEOPLE HATE LAWYERS

The problem of force in ethical decision making has a lot to do with why people hate lawyers. Of course, there are many reasons why people hate attorneys: greed, incompetence, arrogance, duplicity, to name a few. However, I suspect that the most pervasive reason for the hatred of lawyers is that lawyers do the dirty work of society: they force other people to do what they should have done in the first place. In our justice system, the plain and simple truth is that no one takes you seriously until you appear ready to use the ultimate force available to an attorney: go to trial.

For example, in a recent medical malpractice case, I represented the family of a woman who had been turned into a paraplegic by the unmistakable negligence of two sets of Navy physicians in two hospitals, neither of which were communicating about the patient's treatment. One set of physicians was on the East Coast and another on the West Coast. In the years after the surgeries, they had been transferred to various states all over the country. An administrative notice of the family's claim had been filed, but the government would not offer to negotiate the case. Finally, the lawsuit had to be filed in federal district court. It was not until I set the depositions of 20 doctors and other healthcare providers all over the country that the government finally conceded liability and awarded the family the maximum amount allowed by law, $350,000.00 cash plus $4,000.00 per month for the remaining life of the patient for her continuing care.

In the family law arena, as another example, it is the rare parent who voluntarily gives the statutory guideline for child support. Instead, as a general rule, they have to be taken to court at least once to get an adequate amount of support. The truth is that no one wants to admit that they are wrong or that they owe another person money. Inevitably, the force available to plaintiffs by way of trial and execution of judgment must be used. This is probably the main reason why people hate attorneys. The defendants hate us because we force them to admit wrong-doing and to turn over the sums of money that are required by law. Our clients likewise often hate us because they associate with us the struggle to accomplish the task and dislike having to pay legal fees for something that they feel was justly theirs in the first place. In short, people hate attorneys because of human nature: we never want to admit that we are at fault and we usually compensate others for wrongs only when we have been forced to do so.

The same analysis is true in the criminal law context: if a defendant is found guilty, he feels his lawyer has let him down; if he is found not guilty, he hates the lawyer for having to pay him legal fees when he was, after all, innocent. It is a no-win situation. Now you know the main reason that lawyers charge up-front retainers based on the estimate of work to be done in a case.

## America's Addiction To The Wicked Witch

*Ding, dong, the Witch is Dead,*
*the Wicked Witch, the Wicked Witch*
*Ding, Dong, the Wicked Witch Is Dead!*

*The Wizard of Oz*

It has been said that "violence is as American as apple pie." Anyone who has ever watched T.V., read a newspaper or listened to the radio knows this all too well. This nation was in fact born amidst the violent turmoil of the American Revolution. Unfortunately, each one of us is born into a culture of violence, starting with the fables and stories we are told as children. There is also a tragic connection between our addiction to violence and our belief, previously discussed, that evil is something that actually exists. Our fables, stories, folklore and national cultural heritage all tell us that extreme violence is always justified in the face of pure evil. Since we seem collectively to crave violence, then we must justify it by believing in evil.

The truth is that we are trained and conditioned by birth to consider other people evil or wicked without really knowing or understanding anything about their lives, needs or background at all. Recall that in the visual exercise on people you fully understand, no one you really knew was labeled by you as evil! Therefore, our predisposition to label people evil must end before any meaningful reform of our ethical and justice system can begin. We might call it a crusade to end one of America's truly sacred cows: the *Wicked Witch!*

Remember your mixed emotions when you had to finally admit there was no *Santa Claus*? In a similar way, we must now outgrow our childhood addiction to the *Wicked Witch*! I call it an addiction to emphasize the great harm that this fascinating faith has caused us and continues to cause us. Let us review together this powerful theme in one of America's most beloved fables.

Never has the dualism of good versus evil been so potently fabricated. I remember my fear as a child watching the Wicked Witch of the West appear in clouds of fiery smoke, throw fireballs at the helpless Strawman, and ride through the sky on her broomstick, leaving a trail of black smoke writing "Surrender Dorothy!" Watching it again recently I was afraid for a different reason: the fable portrays that absolute evil not only exists, but gives fundamental meaning and direction to our lives!

Although the *Wizard of Oz* has many lighthearted moments, there is nothing but deadly seriousness about the Wicked Witch. No explanation is provided at all for why she is wicked: her evil is an absolute given that must be accepted if Dorothy's adventure is to be enjoyed at all. The Wicked Witch's counterpart in Dorothy's real world also reveals no basis for her evilness, unless not liking to be bitten by dogs and owning "half the county" are indicia of evil. Of course, there could be no explanation of why the Wicked Witch was the way she was: that would humanize her and make her a real person. Instead, her evilness is unquestionable; we know this from the start because, as the "Good Witch" points out, only "bad witches" are ugly and old. In short, we know the Wicked Witch is evil *just by looking at her!*

Tragically for our society, the Wicked Witch becomes the setting, the connecting link, and the ultimate goal for all of Dorothy's adventures...and for all of our adventures. The movie has hardly begun before the real-world Wicked Witch makes her first appearance on an unsightly bicycle. This witch dominates, controls and inspires all the action of the play: her protest at being bitten and wanting Toto put to sleep causes Dorothy to run away from home. Her obsession with the power of the ruby slippers, which Dorothy innocently guards, causes all the violence and drama on the Yellow Brick Road. As for Dorothy's companions, the only way Strawman uses his brain is to outwit the witch. The only way Tinman and Lion show heart and courage is in the struggle against the Wicked Witch. And, ultimately, the only way Dorothy can achieve her homeward goal is to go to the Wicked Witch's castle and bring her broomstick back to the Wizard.

Bring back her broomstick? Why, that would mean, "We will have to kill her," says the inherently intelligent Strawman! And, of course, kill her they do. But in the most noble way. You see, if you are as good and innocent as Dorothy, you just wind up killing the "bad guys/gals" by accident. Remember, Dorothy made her grand debut in Oz by accidently landing on the Wicked Witch's sister. This was followed by the greatest party the Munchkins have ever thrown, in celebration of the fact that she was "really, positively, absolutely, most sincerely...dead!" You see, it's OK to kill truly *wicked* people, especially if it is done by accident!

This early message was not wasted on Dorothy. In the end, she pulls off an even more astonishing feat: she accidently kills the Wicked Witch of the West when she douses Strawman to save him from the witch's fire ball! In the finest American tradition, it's always OK to kill someone if you are rescuing someone else. And, water being pure and associated with such things as baptism, the witch just naturally had to melt on the spot! As she put it, "Who would have thought that a good little girl and her dog could have ended all my beautiful wickedness," just in case anyone doubted whether she had so much as an ounce of human decency in her! You see, *nobody* liked her; even her guards immediately swore allegiance and praise to Dorothy once their evil dominatrix was dead. So Dorothy returns triumphant to the Wizard, having slain the (female) dragon while saving the life of the good Strawman.

Meanwhile, back at Emerald City, she and her companions are then confronted with an even greater challenge: the terrifying, great and magnificent OZ, who knows *all* (sounds like *God* to me!), tells them...to come back tomorrow. The challenge, of course, is to realize that there is no OZ, and that they had merely to discover the wisdom, love and courage that was within them all along. And, it is never too late for even the most wayward prodigal son or daughter to return home...to people they love and the values they hold dear. We cherish that part, a powerful and beautiful message endeared to our hearts for decades. But at a terrible price!

Two dead witches. Somehow or other, after we Americans have come to the rescue, done good deeds or protected our ideals, there usually seem to be some, (often a lot) of dead bodies lying around. They are, of course, not really dead people, just dead bodies. Just like the Wicked Witch. When the water zapped her, it was really her fault she died. Not only did she try to burn Strawman alive, but it was her fault she was susceptible to water. How was Dorothy to know the witch was so inhuman that she didn't even drink water?

Two dead witches is OK because they weren't human. Thank God, however, that Dorothy didn't accidently spill water on the *Good Witch of the North,* unless, perhaps, good witches can enjoy a nice glass of water, at least once in a while!

Enough sarcasm. I trust some humor is in order as we try to dismantle one of America's greatest strangleholds on our moral progress: our firm conviction that the "good" may and must use violent force to triumph over "evil," or phrased otherwise, that deadly force may ultimately be used over the most pure evil. Didn't we all sense, from the beginning, that the Wicked Witch had to go? Imagine the story without the Wicked Witch melting. The witch *had* to die. There could be no joy, no safety, no completion without her death. In order to achieve her most prized goal, her return to home and loved ones, Dorothy had to kill...because there was a Wicked Witch!

As fascinating as the *Wizard of Oz* was for us in our youth, we must put away this naive, childish thinking if we are to advance ethically as a nation. In a new fable for our new century, *The Wizard of Oz 2000,* we won't have Dorothy killing any witches because there will be no witches, good or bad. Does this make for a boring fable? No. The fable is less violent, of course, but certainly not boring. The tale can proceed just as written, simply without the evil and the killing. The search on the Yellow

Brick Road for wisdom, love and courage can be just as thrilling, even if the road does not end in violence and death. Just as Dorothy had to give up the Santa Claus image of the Wizard, so do we all have to give up our most cherished and sacred belief: that some other people are evil and that we must determine who they are and put them to death, whether it be persons within our own culture or an entire nation, such as Iraq, North Vietnam in the 60's or Germany in the 40's.

Unfortunately, unlike Dorothy, in our criminal justice system we don't have the luxury of "accidentally" killing people who commit terrible crimes. We must do one of three things: kill them on purpose, lock them up forever, or provide them the chance to change, which means that, no matter how horrible their crime, we must be able to forgive them. I believe this is one of the great challenges of our moral and ethical thinking for this century. Our task, then, is much like that of the Wizard, who ultimately had to admit that he was *not* a wizard. We Americans are likewise not wizards, and we cannot be the ultimate judge of who must live and die in this country. Instead, these final choices must be left to each person on their own journey, their own "yellow brick road."

You, the reader, may be arguing to yourself that analysis of children's stories of wicked witches has no relevance to the real world or to modern, realistic adult literature and entertainment. Contemporary films, you may say, show a very real need for violence against truly evil people. If you believe this, take the following test. Pick any ten movies which have numerous acts of violence, for example westerns, cops and robbers shows or war films. Record the amount of time spent on the actual life of the "bad guy"—his or her childhood, rearing, and the circumstances of his entire life. Compare that with the amount of time devoted to the life and action of the hero. In virtually every case, you will discover that, like the Wicked Witch of the East, virtually no time is devoted towards understanding the bad guy—his or her evil is *always a given.* Intellectually, our nation's adult entertainment is still back in *Wizard of Oz* fantasy land. Perhaps you will then join me in thinking that the vast majority of films being made today are simply boring repeats of a dead concept...evil!

# Mystery Number 7

## We Are, Paradoxically, Both Responsible And Nonresponsible For Our Actions

*Liberty means responsibility, that is why most men dread it.*

George Bernard Shaw, *Maxims for Revolutionists*

*I do not understand my own actions.
For I do not do what I want,
but I do the very thing I hate.*

Saint Paul's letters, *7 Romans 15*

Imagine that someone approaches you with a large suitcase and opens it before you. It is filled with neatly stacked bundles of hundred dollar bills. He offers you a million dollars if you could, overnight, remake yourself into a 100 percent better person! Could you change so dramatically? How could you accomplish this change? If you are like me, an overnight total overhaul of your whole being is most unlikely! This is obviously because what took 47 years to create is not likely to change radically from one moment to the next!

It is probably abundantly clear to you how you got to be the way you are and have the beliefs that you believe. You also probably cannot imagine yourself actually behaving or acting any differently from the way you normally act and behave. Certainly most people would admit that true change in their lives is both rare and miraculous. The truth is that we cannot fully escape the forces that determine who we are and what we do.

Another equally compelling truth, however, is that we do in fact make choices in our lives. We make choices every day from what we wish to buy to how we wish to occupy our time. And sometimes we make choices with powerful life-enhancing or life-destroying consequences, such as the choice of the Menendez brothers to purchase the shotguns that they later used to murder their parents. In short, we are paradoxically incapable of change, yet we must make choices that affect and change our lives every day.

This is the age-old debate of determinism versus free will. Determinists believe that our actions are always a result of pre-existing factors such as genetic make-up, one's nature and nurturing as a child, and the circumstances in which one is brought up. Under a strictly deterministic viewpoint, people should not be responsible for any of their actions and therefore can never be held accountable or punished, since everything that they do, in essence, is predestined. Obviously, such an approach, if followed, could lead to chaos and lawlessness in our society.

A strict "free will" approach takes the opposite view—that we are totally and without any reservation responsible for every action that we take. Under this view, then, a person is responsible for his conduct despite the circumstances of his actions and personal background. So it would not matter that a person had stolen a loaf of bread if in fact it was the only means to feed his family. And it would not be relevant to their sentencing that the Menendez brothers committed their crimes after a lifetime of criminal abuse by their parents. Clearly, the harshness of this approach is as inhumane as the deterministic approach is irresponsible. And so, our ethical decision making must constantly chart a course between the perils of either extreme.

Let us apply these extreme theories to our three ethical issues. Under a deterministic viewpoint, we are ultimately not responsible for our actions. Put simply, our lives are beyond our control. This is the theoretical basis for an extreme liberal viewpoint. Thus, a woman who gets pregnant is not responsible for getting pregnant and therefore, is entitled to use abortion as a form of birth control. A criminal who commits a heinous offense is ultimately not responsible for what he did, since his acts were a culmination of a tragic childhood and bad DNA/RNA coding. And, finally, if a person is terminally ill, that too, is hardly their fault and they should be entitled to choose death as a means of escaping from the inevitable prolonged pain.

In contrast, if your philosophy is that each person has free will and is ultimately responsible for his actions, then you will follow the conservative approach to each of these issues. A woman who gets pregnant short of rape is responsible for creating another life and may not avoid her responsibility to at least bring the child to full term. A criminal, no matter how pathetic his childhood, is responsible for the pain and agony that he causes other individuals. In certain heinous cases he must pay the ultimate price of death for his crime. And, finally, on the issue of death with dignity, a person is always responsible to continue his life so long as God sees fit for him to endure the pain.

These two sets of extreme ideologies are just that: nondefendable positions that set up rules precluding an ethical case by case evaluation of each situation. You have, hopefully, already found such a simplistic dichotomy to be sadly lacking in value as an ethical guide. We have already dismissed almost any "hard-and-fast" ethical rule as being impractical. For example, there can be no absolute rule regarding all abortions. Who could possibly assert that a woman should have the sole prerogative to abort a fetus at eight months just because she did not like the sex of the child-to-be? On the other hand, who could quarrel with a woman's decision to abort a fetus conceived by being raped by an HIV positive criminal?

Compare also the imposition of the death penalty for someone who committed a murder under extraordinary duress compared to the death penalty for an individual who had vowed repeatedly to commit murders for profit in the future. And, finally, contrast a death-with-dignity statute without any safeguards or restrictions to prevent the suicide of the merely temporarily ill or depressed as opposed to one that clearly limits death with dignity only as a reasoned end to horrible suffering. After such considerations, I have truly come to believe the oft-quoted saying of Neils Bohr: the opposite of one great truth is not a falsehood, but another great truth.

As I have mentioned, the inconsistencies of the "flaming liberal" and the "arch conservative" also reflect two entirely different sets of psychic wounds that we may have endured as children. If you grew up in an environment where you were either under-disciplined or, alternatively, smothered with no chance for control or individuality in your life, you may find yourself among the rank and file of the "flaming liberals," who as adults have as their goal a rebellion against any form of restriction or responsibility imposed upon them.

On the other hand, if your family environment was one where you had to compensate for being emotionally or physically abandoned, or, in the other extreme, you were brought into a restrictive world where nothing could be questioned, you may have evolved into an "arch conservative." As such an adult, your main goal is to impose the maximum amount of restrictions and responsibility upon both yourself and everyone else you know.

This book, however, is not about labeling people as arch conservatives or flaming liberals. Indeed, it is all about not labeling people. If we have sufficient understanding, we will begin to realize that we have all been wounded in different ways as children, and each of us has an ethical quest before us to understand the complexity and uncertainty of our ethical challenges. Understanding how some of us may have been driven to or drawn toward ethical extremes is simply a starting point toward discovering that the ethical truth of a given situation may be fixed somewhere between two or more extreme viewpoints. In fact, what makes a decision ethical is as much the honest soul-searching that goes into the process as it is the discovering and application of the relevant ethical principles. Simply put, ethical decision making is a process, not the application of a fixed formula or the discovery of the "right" rule to apply to a situation. This is why, ethically speaking, the path to salvation is as narrow as "a razor's edge:" we run as great a risk of falling off to "conservative" extremes as to "liberal" extremes. And the salvation of each person rests uniquely with their own soul-searching at every point in our lives. It is, when all is said and done, a journey that we each must travel alone.

# Four Paintings—Four Truths

## When This Ship Leaves, The Land Goes With It!

I painted this canvas to capture the following dream. I take a woman friend on board a ship to impress her with my knowledge of ships and the crew. However, I say something in front of one of the crew that upsets her and she disappears in anger. I look all over the ship for her without success. Then the ship's loudspeaker announces "The ship will depart in 5 minutes—all ashore who are going ashore."

The warning is repeated and I grow more desperate—I must find my friend and leave the ship at once. A sailor notices me and asks what is wrong. I tell him my predicament and he replies, "Don't worry, when this ship leaves, the land goes with it!"

This was, I believe, a manifestation of a childlike desire for the impossible—the resolution of anxiety over a woman by reversing the laws of nature. In my painting, woman, land and sea are also as one, joined together inseparably. There is no clear delineation of flesh or the elements of nature. There is then, no real woman. This female figure is not free, but bound and controlled by the fiery sky and stormy sea of my own subconscious needs. She symbolizes, then, women before emancipation, before being recognized as having a right to own land, vote or control her own body.

## The Flying Swan Duchess

This mythologic, archetypal swan-woman was my first creation of a feminine being of great independence and power. In contrast to *When This Ship Leaves, The Land Goes With It*, this swan-woman is absolutely free and unrestricted as she flies out of the ocean. Beneath the waves she glows as a hot, fertile swan, a symbolic womb over which she has full control as the lower part of her body.

This painting, I believe, manifests my growing understanding of why, in the incredibly difficult issue of the right to life, women should decisively be charged with this ultimate responsibility...and this ultimate power.

## THE UNION

I set out to paint a landscape of the Laguna Mountains in California and instead created this strange painting that I do not fully understand. For me, it seems to reveal a process of relation, between a lighter, more ethereal feminine force on the top, pulling along a heavier masculine force below. The union of the two seems to be a sexual, reproductive coupling.

It also represents very much how ideas are created and decisions formed—a dance between the joys of freedom. . . and the weight of responsibility.

## THE ARRIVAL OF DEATH

One day while driving with a friend across the plains of Arizona, I saw rock formations that looked like ships on the distant horizon. Suddenly I was seized with the sensation that one of these was approaching me. I started sketching the vision, and, as I did, realized that I was drawing...Death! Later I painted that vision as a fierce, all powerful burning force—a reality that must be noticed, respected, and finally, encountered.

I saw Death as something that can be greeted and accepted. It is not something to always fear, or always escape. Rather, it is a part of our lives: the ending, which may be embraced nobly and boldly. I think for many of us, encountering our death can be as thrilling, challenging and powerful a decision as any that we make in our lives.

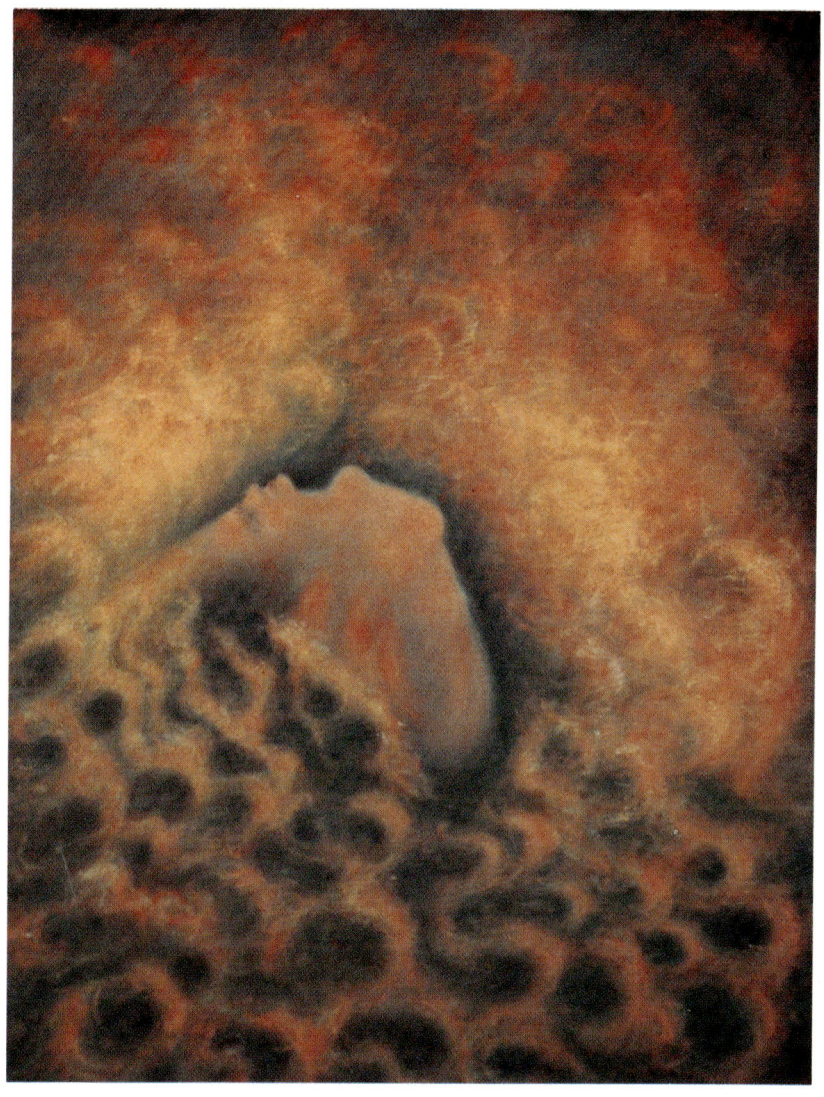

*When this Ship Leaves, the Land Goes With It!*

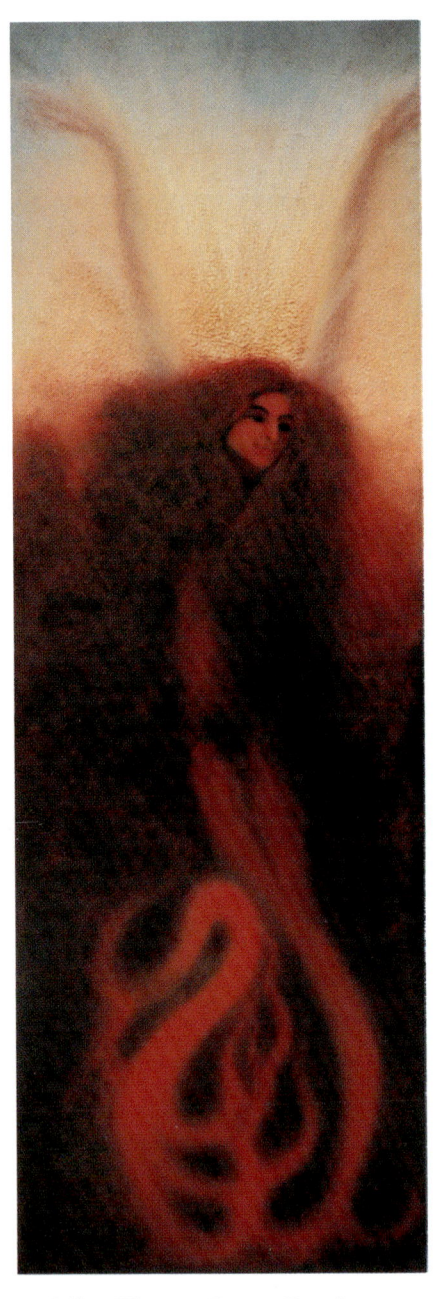

*The Flying Swan Duchess*

*The Union*

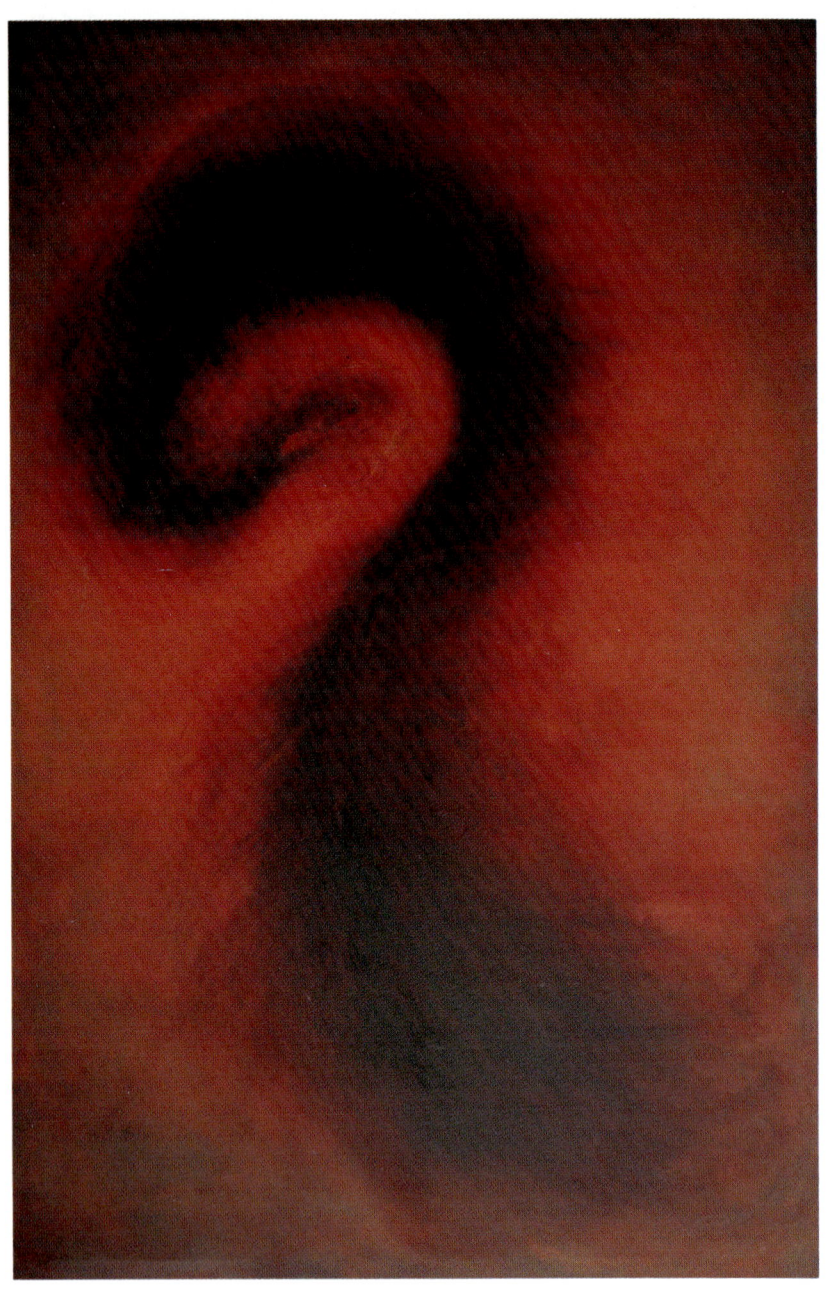

The Arrival of Death

# Part Three

## The Seven Mysteries and The Ethical Dilemmas Of Our Age

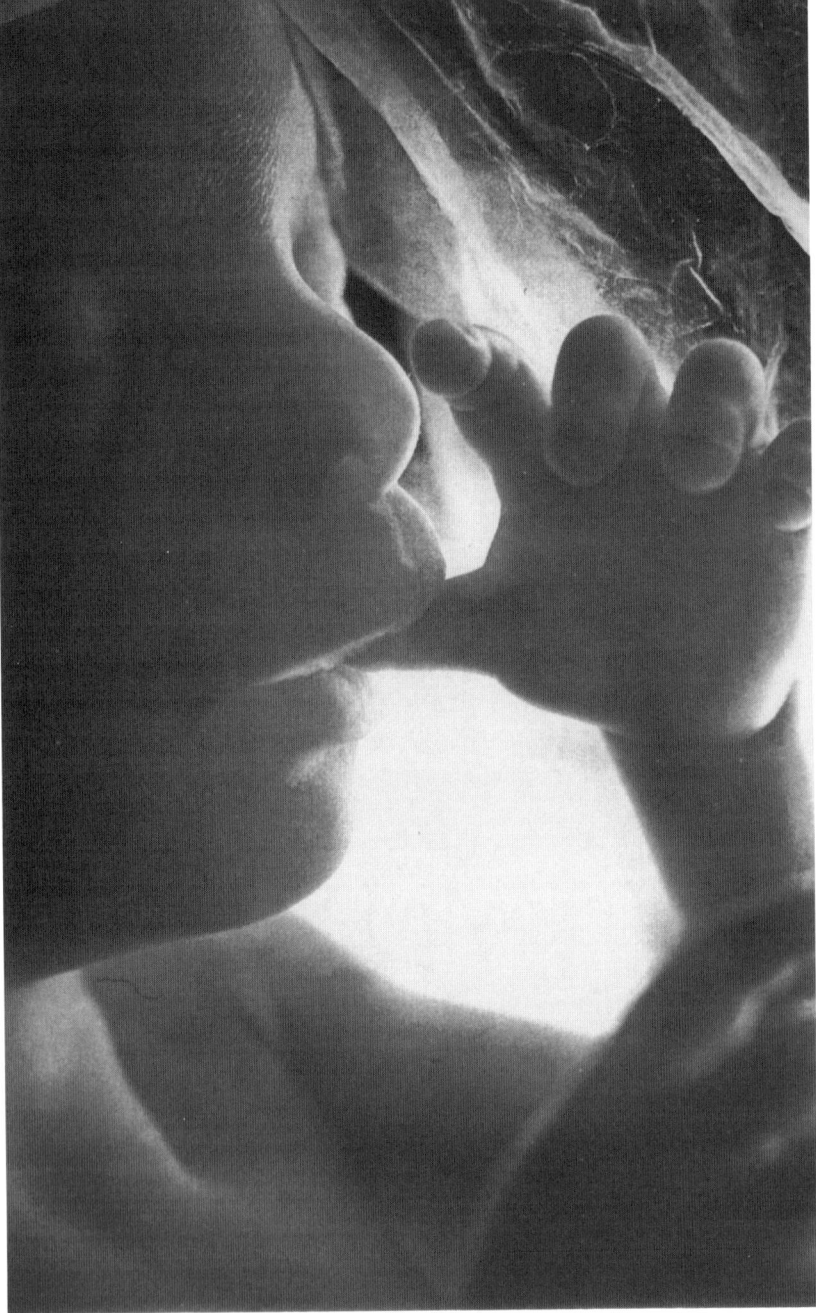

# ABORTION: THE ULTIMATE ETHICAL DILEMMA

The abortion issue involves a staggering number of potential human lives. And, in the past few decades, the number of abortions has escalated dramatically. In 1969 fewer than 25,000 abortions were reported to the Center for Disease Control, an agency of the United States Public Health Service. Four years later in 1972, approximately one half million abortions were reported to CDC. In 1987, approximately 1.3 million abortions were reported to CDC, which meant that there was about one abortion for every three live births in the United States.[25] There have been, therefore, since 1969, literally millions of abortions performed, undoubtedly over thirty million. In "black or white," either/or thinking, there have been either thirty million murders...or thirty million unwanted children saved from a miserable existence.

Without question, the struggle over the abortion issue is currently the most volatile, emotional and politically explosive ethical struggle in this country. We undertake to unravel it first for a number of reasons. First, it involves the ultimate question of when human life comes into meaningful existence. Secondly, it appears to be the most difficult ethical challenge because, unlike other ethical dilemmas, it involves a totally helpless and innocent being, the fetus, who is still in existence at the time the ethical decision must be made. It is, therefore, arguably different from the death penalty issue, where the victims have already been injured prior to the ethical decision of punishment. It also differs from the death with dignity issue for the same reason, that there is no "innocent third party" who will arguably be forever affected by the decision. Although, of course, friends, relatives and loved ones may be permanently affected by the decision in cases involving the death penalty and death with dignity, their loss is not a direct one as is the destruction of a human fetus. As a background to our discussion, let us review the relevant principles we have established so far.

1. The only rule is that there are no "hard-and-fast" rules; that is, we must turn to ethical principles but allow for individual choice given the relative facts and circumstances of a person's life.
2. The broader an ethical principle, the less practical guidance it provides for decision making.
3. Ethical decisions constantly balance our changing needs against the needs of others, since everyone's needs are equally important.
4. It takes a person to make an ethical decision.
5. The concept of "good" versus "evil" is an abstraction that affords no clear basis for ethical decision.
6. Degrees of force are inevitable components of both ethical decision making and ethical principles.
7. We are paradoxically both responsible and not responsible for our actions.

Let us now apply these principles to create the most ethical approach and framework for a person facing the question of abortion.

## CAN THERE BE AN ABSOLUTE RULE REGARDING ABORTION?

The abortion issue seems to be one peculiarly beset by the "all-or-nothing" mentality of our political, cultural and religious environment. Politicians who favor the woman's right to choose are labeled evil butchers, likened to the German Nazis in World War II. In contrast, pro-choicers see right wing pro-lifers as having no real concern for helping living human beings, but only concern about ensuring that people "pay" for having sex. However, it takes little sophistication to realize that either extreme position is ethically invalid. Consider the photograph of a sixteen-week old fetus; this type and quality of picture was not available until recently. It has been only in the recent past that we have understood the full extent to which a fetus was developed at that point of gestation. No one is going to seriously come forward and say that a woman should have an absolute and unfettered right to choose to abort a fetus at that age, simply because, for example, she does not like the sex of the child. A fetus, at that age, is a sacred and beautiful creation that merits the right to life. Surely no one can claim that all abortions are ethically permissible no matter when they occur and no matter what the reason.

On the other hand, there are many worse horrors than never having been born. Consider the people on death row. Virtually all of the men and women facing execution came into this world amidst a parade of all kinds of abuse: physical, emotional, sexual, often combined and worsened from drug and alcohol addiction inherited from their parents. Undoubtedly for these people, it would have been better if they had never been born. So if a mother feels that she is unable to rear and bring a child into this world, who can say that she is not doing the most loving thing by choosing an abortion?

One need only read the local newspaper a few days in a row to see children dying from all types of parental neglect. In Oakland, California, three children died when fire engulfed their family's apartment, which their mother had lit by candles because the electricity had been turned off.

In another case, a young child was killed by a rat as he slept in a car with his parents. The mother and father were so drugged that they did not hear the cries of the child as it was eaten alive!

Another way children ultimately die from parental neglect is directly connected with our second ethical issue: the death penalty. Almost all of the men and women facing the death penalty had horrific childhoods. When they are finally caught and convicted of a heinous murder, they often wish to die rather than continue living. On the next page is the picture of Wayne Lee Bates, who at one time was scheduled to be the first person killed in Tennessee's electric chair in thirty-three years.[26] He murdered a woman after a history of child abuse and childhood addiction to drugs and alcohol. He had become an alcoholic by the age of six. At one appellate hearing, his request to fire his lawyer, dismiss all appeals, and accept the death sentence was granted. In response to letters urging him to fight for his life, he replied, "Where were you when I needed you? Where were you when I could maybe have changed? Where were you? I cry a lot."[27] Clearly, for this young man, he would have been better off never having been born. Would you choose to come into existence if such was your fate?

If the state of California is used as an example, at least half of all convicted murderers on death row give up their fight to remain alive. Of the two men executed by California since 1967 to the present, one of them, David Mason fired his previous attorney and hired attorney Michael K. Brady to keep his execution date from appeals by death penalty opponents. Attorney Brady suffered severe criticism for reversing the normal role of a defense lawyer in protecting his client's right to choose death. The previous attorney's appeal contended that severe childhood abuse rendered Mason incapable of informed decision concerning his desire to die. Finally, Mason got his wish—he was executed on August 23, 1993, thirteen years after committing the robbery-murders of four elderly people.

Sometimes children take the law into their own hands because of abuse by their parents.

Recently, there has been a series of children charged with the murder of their parents. In Rush Springs, Oklahoma, a father

# Murderer Ready For Electric Chair

■ 'Lawyers are making my life miserable, all they can do is postpone the execution for a year,' Bates says.

Wayne Lee Bates, 35, is slated to be the first prisoner killed in Tennessee's electric chair in 33 years. Governer Ned McWherter has alerted the Department of Corrections to excute Bates on December 1, unless the state receives orders from the court.

was murdered by his teenage boys, who in their own words, were merely following their father's instructions: "If anyone ever messes with (sister) Sissy, hit him behind the ear or in the heart. Kill him!" According to a *Los Angeles Times* article, the Dutton case was one of three parricides during the past year in Oklahoma, "a state with social workers scrambling to keep up with 26,300 reports of child abuse filed that year."[28]

The point is simply this: if abortions had not been legal for the past twenty years, among the thirty million or so additional new lives brought into this country, there would be many more millions of young children unlovingly brought into a world of abuse, abandonment and eventual crime or victimization. If only 10 percent of these potential unwanted lives had turned into criminals, our country would be beset with three million more felons added to our already crime-ridden cities and swollen jails. From my own experience as a defense attorney, however, I would estimate the percentage to be much higher. What would our nation be like today if half of these unwanted children turned to crime, giving us fifteen million more felons?

Certainly no child should be brought into a world of abuse, filth and victimization. And consider the hypothetical fact of a woman raped by a man with AIDS. Virtually no one, even the most extreme pro-lifers, would claim that the fetus should be brought into such a miserable and tragic life. Clearly, then, there can be no absolute rules on the issue of abortion. Yet, at the same time, both individuals and society need principles to guide them when faced with the dilemma of abortion.

Our task, in building an ethical framework to address the abortion question, is to provide guidelines that allow for individual choice as applied to the facts of each person's situation. What then should those principles be?

## Balancing The Rights And Needs Of The Mother, The Fetus And Society

If there can be no absolute rules regarding abortion, then we are left with a precarious and unsettling task of balancing the rights and needs of the mother, the fetus and society. As a generalization, all three have equally compelling and vital rights and needs. A fetus, at any stage of development, is a living, growing, potential child and ordinarily should enjoy the right to come into existence. A mother, on the other hand, enjoys the conflicting right of privacy and control over her own body. Finally, society has the right and the duty to ensure that the rights and needs of the unborn children, the privacy of women, and the needs of society are respected to the extent mutually possible.

This balancing calls into question the difficult issue of when life begins. In a strictly simplistic fashion, if you believe that life begins upon conception, you readily reach the conclusion that no abortion is ethical or legal, since the taking of a fetus' life as so defined would be murder. On the other hand, a facile definition of life as beginning only upon the taking of the child's first breath leads one easily to the conclusion that all abortions are legal. Obviously, neither simplistic approach satisfies the need to balance the competing interests and rights of the fetus and the mother.

In his excellent work, "Life's Dominion: An Argument on Abortion and Euthanasia," author Ronald Dworkin explains that the difference between pro-choicers and pro-lifers is their understanding of what constitutes life itself. Pro-choicers are more likely to understand life as the appreciation, enhancement and value of a child that results from his being raised and nurtured upon birth. Pro-lifers on the other hand, see life as a given: a fetus already has all of its potential qualities of living upon conception. This dichotomy is reminiscent of the free will v. determinism debate we discussed in the previous chapter. Do children come into this world with predetermined characteristics, or are their personalities more the product of their nurturing and the choices made in their lives? As with that debate, the question of when life begins has no ready answer. However, if the very purpose and meaning of life is to be able to love and to be loved by others, we are provided some general guidance as to where the line in any given case should be drawn between the rights of the fetus and the rights of the mother.

If love is the fundamental basis of life, the potential life should be one where a child would receive the benefit of being loved and could acquire the capacity to love. Since an unwanted fetus would in most cases become an unwanted child, a powerful argument exists for preventing children who would be unloved, unwanted and uncared for from coming into existence. As argued before, there is a connection between this phenomenon and the reality within the criminal justice system that, almost invariably, criminal defendants come from families where the children were neither loved nor wanted. In my own experience as a Navy criminal defense attorney my clients had, almost without exception, come from dysfunctional or non-existent families where they were unloved and mistreated. Thus, an ethic that would allow for abortions in these cases would also promote a goal of the criminal justice system, that is, decreasing the number of people likely to commit crimes.

Of course, the most meaningful and effective solution to the abortion problem is to prevent the need for them in the first place. The emphasis should be on preventing these problems, not on resolving them once they occur. There should be more public education concerning birth control and the responsibilities of parenthood. Nevertheless, realistically, there will always be those who, either through their own irresponsibility or as a result of themselves being victims of violence, have unwanted pregnancies. I am concerned here with our ethical guidelines and institutions in the cases of pregnancy which in fact occur. I also believe that free and available adoption services should be provided to those women who realize that they cannot care for their own child but who choose not to end its existence.

In any event, when an unwanted pregnancy occurs, the woman and society are faced with the question of what to do. Clearly, the rights and needs of the mother must be balanced against the rights and needs of the fetus as it develops. At any given time in the fetus' development, a decision must be made and, inevitably, what that decision will be is inextricably bound up with the question of who will make that decision.

## WHO MUST MAKE THE DECISION?

When an unwanted pregnancy occurs, who is in the best position to determine whether the baby should be born? Who can best decide whether the child would be in fact loved, cared for and raised, so that the child could become a loving, caring and giving person? What person or persons can best see the most accurate and truthful paradigm; that is, who can choose between the vision of the child brought up to become a happy and fulfilled member of society or a child destined to become involved in crime and to create misery for other innocent people? The answer must inevitably be the person closest in every way to that fetus and the person whom our society charges with the most intimate nurturing and rearing of the child. That is, of course the child's mother. As the slogan goes, "If you can't trust the woman with the choice, how can you trust the woman with the (rearing of the) child?"

To entrust this ultimate decision with the mother is clearly not to say that "all abortions are right" or that "abortions are inherently ethical," for there are obviously many instances where an abortion would be unethical and immoral: for example, the case where abortion is used as a means of controlling the sex of a couple's child. Obviously, few would take issue with a rule that made it a crime to abort a fetus because of the sex of the child, although such a rule would be difficult to enforce. Ultimately, the issue is one of trust: who does society trust to limit abortions only where the woman is clearly incapable of either bringing the child to full term or raising and loving the child in a competent manner? For me and for most people in this country, the logical and inevitable answer is the person most charged with the responsibility for raising the child, namely, the mother.

Another reason for giving this ultimate decision to the mother is that women's moral sense is usually more naturally attuned to the realms of relationships and nurturing, two key considerations in the question of abortion. In his recent book, *The Moral Sense*, James Q. Wilson reveals that "men and women differ in their moral orientation." He concludes, along with many other researchers, that while men tend to emphasize "justice, fairness and duty," women are more likely to stress "sympathy, care and helping."[29] This seems clear and obvious to me, and it suggests a conclusive reason why the woman must be given the abortion decision. If the woman senses that she will be unable to love and nurture the child, she is probably right that the child would not, in fact, be loved or wanted.

A final and most compelling reason for giving the woman the decision concerning abortion is that it is, after all is said and done, her body and her life that is involved. This is a reality that men in a male-dominated, patriarchal culture have the greatest difficulty in grasping. Our society has great reluctance to empower women with both the power to create life, and the power to impose death upon the unwanted fetus. Yet, this is a power that other cultures have readily and fully granted women, out of the necessity of ensuring that all children come into this world wanted, protected, and nurtured during infancy.

The famous lecturer and author Ginette Paris has expressed this reality eloquently by calling upon the dual powers of Artemis, the Greek goddess who was both the protector of wild animals and the hunter of them, and who was called upon by women both during the pains of labor and to invoke a quick and merciful death if a woman or infant could not survive. She writes that a woman must be called upon to say no if she senses that the birth of a fetus is not morally justified:

> Artemis stands for the refusal to give life if the gift is not pure and untainted, whether it be by the domination of one sex over another or by conditions that make it anything but joyful. A mother who never learns to say 'no', 'stop,' and 'enough' threatens her child's well-being; the same principle applies from the moment of conception. To say 'no' is a fundamental aspect of being maternal. It is more than limit-setting. It is an insight coming from Artemis that 'no' is basic to life and the survival of the planet. Those who claim that abortion today is an indication of selfishness on the part of women and couples, that the child is sacrificed to the lowest standards of our atheistic materialism, express a certain aspect of the problem, because egoism and materialism certainly do exist. But by looking closely at individual cases a more important theme emerges: the majority of women who abort do so because they know that the unwelcome child, born of constraint and misfortune, will be wounded in some unacceptable way. As Artemis might kill a wounded animal rather than allow it to limp along miserably, so a mother wishes to spare the child a painful destiny. There is nothing more cruel than the suffering of children, and mothers know this better than anyone.[30]

If women are not given the final decisional power, who or what authority would have it? An alternative mechanism would be to place the issue in the family court system. Already overworked and understaffed, family court judges would have added to their burdens not only the task of determining what was in the best interests of children in divorce issues of custody and visitation, but the impossible decision of what was in the best interest of the fetus. How could a judge make a valid and meaningful determination in such cases? As in juvenile court proceedings, the fetus could be appointed an attorney who would make an immediate examination of the facts, along with a court-appointed social worker, to determine if the request to abort the fetus was based on the proper principles of the capacity to care for the child versus some clearly unethical and immoral purpose, such as sex determination.

I can think of no greater litigation nightmare, since proving or disproving the real motivation of the parent would be virtually impossible. In addition, the cost of such a system would be astronomical. Finally, the judicial system is inherently incapable of moving with the speed that such decisions require. Accordingly, the inescapable conclusion is that, just as we must ultimately trust mothers to raise and rear their children properly, we must also trust the women with this ultimate decision whether to bring their children into the world in the first place.

## SHOULD THE FATHER HAVE ANY SAY?

If women have a right to abortion, do men have an equivalent right? Should the potential father have any say in whether the fetus is brought to term or not? The idea of forcing a woman either to have an abortion or not have one is repugnant to the privacy and autonomy of women. Clearly, a father cannot require a mother to have an abortion. But can he prevent one? In its 1992 opinion of *Planned Parenthood v. Casey,* the Supreme Court summarily dismissed the notion that the father of a fetus must be informed or give consent for the abortion to occur.[31] This is as it should be, since the father's wanting to have the child come to term will not alone change whether the mother feels capable of bringing the fetus to term or raising the child. Clearly, then the father should have no ultimate power either to require an abortion or to prevent one.

However, in cases of pregnancy out of wedlock, should the woman alone have the decisional power to obligate the father financially for eighteen years of a potential child's life? Is it fair to impose upon him the requirement to financially support the child if he is not in agreement that the child should be brought to term? In all fairness, why should the pregnant woman have the only control in this situation? One logical resolution of this issue is to give the woman the sole control on the question of bringing the child to term, but impose upon the father of the child born out of wedlock the responsibility to support the child only if he has been given notice and has consented to the bringing of the child into the world. This issue needs to be examined by our legislatures to reach some workable compromise on the respective rights and duties of men and women.

Under the present system, the biological father is always financially responsible to support the child, whether it is born in or out of wedlock. This has had the effect of perhaps making men more careful about precautions during sex and has had the beneficial result of supporting children financially. However, to give men and women equal authority and control in the question of a child conceived out of wedlock, I would propose that a woman who wishes to hold a man responsible to financially support a child born out of wedlock must first give him legal notice that she claims to be pregnant by him. Then the putative father can either consent or not to bringing the child to full term. If he does not consent, he will not be held financially responsible for the child. However, he also will have no authority either to require the mother to bring the child to full term or to obtain an abortion. This position is one publicly espoused by such noted feminists as Ginette Paris, and it is one that equally empowers men and women concerning the financial responsibility for raising children born out of wedlock.

## Abortion As Neither "Good" Nor "Evil"

If we entrust women with the ultimate power to decide the fates of their fetuses, we inevitably expose ourselves and our society to both anxiety and uncertainty. Without any hard-and-fast rules concerning abortion, we do not know what must be done in any given case. Yet, this is the very reality of ethics and ethical decision making that we have already discovered. What is moral, right and ethical for one woman or one set of parents in one situation will not be right, moral and ethical in another set of facts. And, as I argued earlier, even within the same set of external circumstances, ethical decisions may vary based on the mental makeup and emotional strength of the mother. We as a society must be prepared to live with this degree of uncertainty if we are to allow for the greatest number of truly ethical decisions, based on the balance between the freedom to choose and the ethical guideline calling for the nurturing and protection of innocent children. In short, the decision to bring or not to bring a child into the world is ethical or not, depending on the circumstances and motivation of the involved parents.

This analysis may be of little consolation to those who see termination of the existence of fetuses as inherently immoral and evil in all cases. To those readers I would argue that just because it may be unethical in some cases, does not mean that it must be in all cases. Even the far right allows for abortion in the case of rape. Furthermore, even the far right is left with the ethical decision of who determines this ultimate decision in cases of rape or to preserve the life of the mother.

Consider also what would happen if we actually prohibited all abortions under any circumstances. Aside from the fact that this is politically unacceptable in this country at this time, such a rule would lead to the disastrous result of young women attempting their own abortions or obtaining abortions from people of doubtful levels of competence. This would lead to many medical disasters to young women, as occurred in the past. Consider also the specter of doctors and other health care providers being prosecuted criminally for assisting women in abortions. The great difficulties generated by proscribing abortions is further proof of why our rules must be flexible in the first place.

Finally, since virtually no one suggests that women who have been raped should be denied access to an abortion, how would it be possible to distinguish between true and falsified cases of rape? Certainly, if that were the only grounds for receiving an abortion, many women might be driven to make a false claim of rape in order to obtain an abortion. No matter what the method of analysis or argument, the most workable solution to the ethical dilemma posed by the abortion problem is to put ultimate faith and trust in the decision of the women involved. It is they who have to carry the fetus full term or not. It is the women who have to undergo the unique pain and risk to their health of the delivery. And, it is the women, often unaided by the fathers, who must ultimately bare the emotional and financial challenge of raising and rearing the children. Inevitably, in the final analysis, it must be their decision.

## THE ETHICAL VALIDITY OF THE USE OF FORCE IN ABORTION

What more forceful or violent act is there than the act of destroying a fetus? In the case of an early termination during the first trimester, a cannula is inserted through the cervical canal into the uterus. Then the fetus is literally suctioned out through the cannula. However, the standard technique used for second trimester abortions is dilation and evacuation (D&E). The dilation for the procedure begins with insertion of laminaria, sticks of compressed seaweed that expand and dilate the cervix. At the beginning of the procedure, the doctor removes the laminaria, then cuts away the fetus with forceps and scraps the walls of the uterus with a curette, a razor-sharp instrument. Clearly, this is as unmistakable an application of physical force as imaginable. The visual brutality of it has been brought home on hundreds of occasions by abortion clinic protesters across the nation.

Whether however, to label a particular abortion an act of force versus an act of violence is simply another way of describing the act as ethical or unethical. The point is that, just because the act involves extreme force, it is not necessarily unethical. If that were true, all operations of any kind for any purpose whatsoever would be unethical. And, if all extreme force was always unethical, the restraint of convicted prisoners, the death penalty and all wars would be, by definition, unethical. I am merely saying that an absolute rule precluding the use of all extreme force in all cases is obviously unworkable and of no use as a meaningful guideline for our ethical conduct. Accordingly, the definitive force used to accomplish an abortion does not by itself make it immoral or unethical.

## ABORTION AND PERSONAL RESPONSIBILITY

One of the mysteries or paradoxes of ethical decision making is that we are both responsible and nonresponsible for our actions, and the best ethical solution to any ethical problem will lie somewhere along the infinite variations between these two extremes. Except for cases where a woman has been raped, both the mother and the father must bear ultimate responsibility for the pregnancy. A strict conservative viewpoint would make the woman in all cases short of rape responsible to bring the child into the world, and a strictly liberal approach would allow a woman to abort a child at any time for any reason. Obviously, both extremes are nontenable. How then can we provide a means to reach this determination in each and every case?

If we have concluded that the only practical resolution is to allow the woman to decide, it follows that only she can make the decision of the extent to which she can be responsible for the rearing of the child. What advantage can there be in attempting to impose responsibility upon a person who has acted irresponsibly in the first place? That would be somewhat akin to asking a person to pull themselves up by their own bootstraps. An individual woman's assessment of her capacity to bring a child to term and to thereafter raise it...is clearly a self-fulfilling prophecy. If she thinks that she can do it, she probably can and, likewise, if she feels incapable of doing it, she will be right on that score as well. Ultimately then, the decision concerning abortion is one that clearly reflects the way Shakespeare phrased all ethical decision making: there is nothing either good or bad but thinking makes it so. Inevitably the abortion decision, at least in the initial stages of pregnancy, is with the woman and the woman alone. Indeed, it is a sacred decision of religious dimension, as eloquently expressed by Ginette Paris:

> Anti-abortion groups impose their values on the overall community on the pretext of holding sacred religious beliefs. We can respond by invoking another moral standard which is just as sacred—respect for the mother/child connection. Because this relationship is the most intimate of all relationships and because a woman's womb is sacred, it is an unacceptable moral violation to force any woman to carry and raise a child against her will. It's a very serious matter to damage this sacred link right at the beginning of life because the seeds of bitterness are sown at a time when love and receptivity are called for. Forcing a child to live in a body that is hostile to it must be denounced as cruel. Is there a less promising way to come into the universe? Life is too precious to allow sexist or religious hostilities to poison the very first stage. The purity of the child calls for an unambivalent response on our part to bring forth each single new life.[32]

The question of responsibility, however, takes on an added dimension when the fetus has reached the point of viability. If the woman, for whatever reason, has allowed or chosen to let the fetus reach that stage in its existence, society must then intervene to protect the fetus. The mother must then assume the additional responsibility to bring the child to term whether she then wants to or not. This is the logical point in which the responsibility of the state to intervene to protect all potential life takes precedence over the rights and decision making of the mother or father. Of course, this is precisely the distinction the Supreme Court has made, both in its initial landmark decision *Roe v. Wade* and in its later amplification of that decision in the more recent case of *Planned Parenthood v. Casey.*

# THE CONTINUING ETHICAL VALIDITY OF *ROE VERSUS WADE* AND LATER SUPREME COURT CASES

With these principles in mind, let us consider the landmark decision of *Roe v. Wade,* decided by the United States Supreme Court in 1973.[33] The genius and moral breakthrough of this decision was that it accommodated the principles we have discussed and created a legal framework by which individuals can apply these principles to the circumstances of their own lives. First, it provided a clear guideline for when the right of privacy of the mother takes precedence over the fetus' right to come into existence. A trimester system was established as follows:

   a. For the stage prior to approximately the end of the first trimester, the abortion decision and its effectuation must be left to the medical judgment of the pregnant woman's attending physician.

b. For the stage subsequent to approximately the end of the first trimester, the State, in promoting its interest in the health of the mother, may, if it chooses, regulate the abortion procedure in ways that are reasonably related to maternal health.

The court further established the third trimester upon which the rights of the fetus to come into existence takes precedence over the woman's right of privacy to choose whether she will bring the child to full term.

c. For the stage subsequent to viability, the State in promoting its interest in the potentiality of human life may, if it chooses, regulate, and even proscribe, abortion except where it is necessary, in appropriate medical judgment, for the preservation of the life or health of the mother.[34]

The mother then is empowered within the first trimester to determine the fate of the fetus; thereafter, only her doctor may abort the fetus if required by the mother's health. Finally, in the third trimester, the doctor may abort the fetus only to save the mother's life.

The *Roe* decision sets forth no absolute rules or guidelines to influence a woman's decision during the first trimester. Wisely, I believe, the ultimate trust to make loving decisions was given to the women of this country. But it does set forth subsequent restrictions, namely taking away the right to abortion in the third trimester, except "for the preservation of the life or health of the mother."

The ethical power of the *Roe v. Wade* decision is that, as the fetus becomes older, the basis on which an abortion is permitted is increasingly limited, thus honoring the conflicting ethical principles that a mother should be able to choose whether she is capable of raising the child and the principle that all life is sacred and must be preserved.

There are, however, no more definitive guidelines for a woman to follow. Particularly in the first trimester, it is ultimately left to the woman's judgment, as it logically must. Each woman must discover, through the journey of her own conscience, whether, under her particular circumstances, she will have the capacity to promote the child's love and happiness without substantially sacrificing her own life. Undoubtedly, most women will make the most loving decision considering her situation, while there will also be some who abuse their power over the fetus' life. In the end, we are left with an imperfect system, but I believe the overall results will be more ethically fulfilled by allowing for these choices.

In recent years there was considerable speculation that the Supreme Court would directly overrule *Roe v. Wade*. However, in June 1992, the Supreme Court decided *Planned Parenthood v. Casey*,[35] which in a five to four vote reaffirmed the holding of *Roe v. Wade*, which they described as "the right of the woman to choose to have an abortion before viability and to obtain it without undue interference from the State." The court therefore upheld the right of a woman to elect abortion, but limited it to the period before fetal viability outside the womb, as opposed to the trimester system in *Roe v. Wade*. In addition, the court set forth a constitutional prohibition from placing an "undue burden" on a woman's decision to abort. Clearly, however, the court allowed for far greater governmental restriction, instruction and interference in the woman's decision making. The court found the following restrictions not to be undue burdens.

1. A 24-hour waiting period, during which a physician must inform the mother of the nature of the abortion procedure and the age of the fetus.

2. A requirement that the woman be informed of the availability of State-published materials describing the fetus and providing information regarding medical assistance for child birth.

3. Adoption or other abortion alternatives.

4. A regulation prohibiting an unemancipated minor under 18 from obtaining an abortion absent consent by at least one parent or a finding by a Judge either that the child is mature and capable of giving informed consent or that an abortion would be in the child's best interest.[36]

Throughout its opinion, the court found that the government possesses a legitimate interest in protecting potential life and in seeking to persuade women to choose childbirth over abortion. The opinion also acknowledged the government's interest in educating women about the physical and psychological health risks of abortion to avoid ill-considered judgements.

Since one goal of all ethical decision making is to base decisions on as much information, analysis and reasoning as possible, I personally am in support of the *Casey* opinion. It leaves the ultimate decision of whether to abort or not in the hands of the woman and certainly nothing is lost and everything is gained by providing the woman with medical information, reasonable alternatives and support should she choose to bring the child to full term. Again, the Supreme Court has created a framework and allowed for a legislative system that affords a woman the maximum amount of information and alternatives before she makes the ultimate decision to abort or not. As in the past, the final decision is left with the person with the most intimate knowledge of whether she could actually promote the child's love and happiness without sacrificing her own life. We are left with a system that cannot possibly satisfy those of us clamoring for an absolute rule regarding abortion. It is instead a system designed to allow for individual choice and, inevitably, individual error as well. Yet it is a system that in the end will allow for the greatest good to occur within our nation.

*Rembrandt*, Abraham Sacrificing Isaac. *1635*

# Criminal Justice And The Death Penalty: The Ultimate Separation From Society

Cultural anthropologists have described one civilization in which fear of evil was an overwhelming preoccupation of the people. It was the belief of that society that evil should be appeased by sacrifices of young men. These men were selected at a very early age, usually at age 17, 18, or 19. They were then examined by priests, who determined if they were the chosen ones to be sacrificed. The priests, over the years, would examine the youths to see if they carried the worst manifestation of the evil within them. Only one out of many thousands would be deemed the truly evil ones. Once they were determined to be carrying the true evil, they were locked in cages for many years. Around the 13th year, if all the priests were in agreement, the boy, then a young man, would be taken to a secret altar where only a chosen few were allowed. Then he would be slain, so that the God of Justice would bless the people and make the society peaceful and orderly.

Of course, this civilization is the present day United States of America! This fanciful story actually describes the way the death penalty is carried out in this country, and it reveals why there must be a change in our criminal justice system, as we shall see.

## Separation As Punishment

In the spring of 1993, I had the honor of participating in a men's workshop led by Shepard Bliss, a founding father of the men's mythopoetic movement. All the men who had volunteered to be small group facilitators were required to be at a training session at our church by 7 P.M. one evening. The group started with introductions, chants and sharing to bring the training staff together as a whole to prepare for the weekend workshop. In just a short time, there was a feeling of energy and purpose in the sanctuary. Then came a knock on the back door. One of the trainers went to let in a latecomer, who took a seat in the circle. There was some discussion between Shepard and his co-leaders. Then Shepard confronted the latecomer and admonished him: "The group cannot go back to repeat all that has happened just for you, so you must leave." There was a moment of painful tension and embarrassment, as each man weighed the consequences of the latecomer's banishment. I remember at first feeling terribly uncomfortable about Shepherd's order. We had all come to help, but this volunteer was being turned away. Slowly, the man realized he was in fact being told to leave. He got up and walked out, no doubt feeling the awful sting of this rebuke as he traveled the long distance to the sanctuary doors.

The training session immediately continued, but, eventually one man felt compelled to question this harsh action: was it really necessary, since this man was a willing volunteer? Shepard replied, "The energy and progress that has been created by the group can not be sacrificed for one man." Equally important, he added, was that the man "got the lesson he came for." Then the friend who had invited him joined in, "Yes, he is invariably late for everything, even when we get together." There was a sense of relief in the room, and a conviction that the "tough love" bestowed upon the late brother was, in fact, just what both he and the group needed. After the explanation was given, I left feeling completely "right" about this "punishment:" it was abundantly clear that this was both a fair and loving decision. Although it involved a relatively minor transgression and correction, the experience was an "ah-ha" revelation for me: love and punishment *can* go hand-in-hand.

Without question, this tough love is what is needed in the criminal justice system. Men and women are degraded if they are not held responsible for their actions and, ultimately, for their lives. But the final goal of most punishment must be to welcome the person back to the common society of men and women. In the case of the latecomer, he was welcome to attend the workshop that weekend, but not as a small group facilitator. That man in fact did attend the workshop and undoubtedly got more out of the experience than if he had been initially excused and accepted by the group. The lesson was unmistakable: as in all the other ethical arenas, force, tempered by love, is an inherent part of justice.

If the purpose of life is to love and be loved, then the question for each criminal is what type and duration of punishment is most likely to achieve the desired result: namely, a more loving person. As was true of the latecomer, virtually all serious offenses still require "punishment" in the form of some separation from society. However, separation from society by itself is not enough. If the separation, whether it be imprisonment, honor camp or some lesser form of restraint, is not made with the goal of the return of the person to society, it may be useless. Although we could count on the late-coming volunteer to use the time away to reflect on why he was late, it is certainly expecting too much to hope that the typical criminal offender will have the emotional and mental capacity to use imprisonment as a time of spiritual and psychological rehabilitation. Unfortunately, the statistics establish that our correctional facilities actually do the reverse of what they are supposed to do: instead of creating a place for rehabilitation where offenders return as better members of society, our prisons are a breeding ground for further criminal activities. They are in fact schools for crime, where young men go to be trained and reinforced in their criminal activity by older and more hardened criminals.

The statistics are frightening and discouraging. The percentage of repeat offenders is about seventy-five percent for most penal institutions. For most of the criminals, then, prison is merely a revolving door.[37]

This recidivism rate, coupled with the increasing percentage of young people involved in the criminal justice system, makes our justice system an undeniable failure. Per capita, the United States imprisons more of its population than virtually any other nation in the world. In 1993, a record high of 948,881 prisoners had been sentenced, a 7.4 percent increase over the previous year. The increase from 1980 to 1993 was about 188 percent.[38]

The problem of the large number of persons imprisoned is compounded in two respects. First, crime is essentially a young man's game. Over ninety percent of all persons in prison for crime are male. Over half of the males arrested are under twenty-five years of age. Twenty-nine percent are under the age of eighteen.[39] We are, therefore, imprisoning many of our youth when instead they should be going to school or trained for a vocation. Secondly, the rate of crime is racially disproportionate. It has been documented for many years that fully 33 percent of all black male youths are in some way involved in the criminal justice system.[40] That is, one out of every three black young men are either being prosecuted, imprisoned or held on probation at any given time! This is a devastating fact of our urban reality. Unless this direction in our society is changed, a dangerously large portion of primarily young men in this nation will be caught up in a life of crime, prosecution and more crime.

There is, of course, no simple solution to this problem. Patterns of parental abuse, neglect and patterns of drug involvement cannot be changed and will not be changed overnight. However, we know what does not work. Although "stiffer," i.e., longer, sentences have become the political fashion of the day, and criminal sentences have become increasingly longer, particularly in the case of drugs, the amount of drug involvement and violent criminal activity has not decreased. Tough love does not mean throwing away the key for extended periods of time without any thought of what the person would be like when they finally leave prison.

How then can the criminal justice system be changed to become more effective? Let us turn to the ethical principles we have discussed before.

## CRIMINAL SENTENCES MUST BE BASED ON BOTH THE FACTS AND THE PERSON... NOT ABSOLUTE RULES.

While I was stationed at the Navy Legal Service Office in San Diego, California, I was assigned to defend one of five sailors at Balboa Naval Hospital accused of an unusual drug conspiracy. They were charged with stealing cocaine by diluting the amount of cocaine in the pain killer given to dying cancer patients! This was hardly a crime that would appeal to the sense of mercy of a typical Navy jury! My defendant, however, was a "walk-on-water" sailor, husband and father. From the onset, I sensed that he sincerely regretted his criminal involvement. In fact, he had already made a full confession to Naval Investigation Service agents. I decided the best option was to follow through with his repentance: plead guilty and offer to give testimony concerning his co-conspirators.

At my client's trial, the jury awarded him only a bad conduct discharge with no confinement whatsoever! I was astonished. We had even asked the jury to award substantial confinement if the jury would keep him in the Navy. Apparently, the jury's thinking was to just get this misfit out of the Navy but reward him for his repentance.

The other co-conspirators fought their prosecutions, but were all convicted. They each received confinement at hard labor varying from several years up to eight years!

Although I was proud of the service I had rendered my client, I was also upset by the enormous disparity in the sentencing. Why should individuals who committed essentially the same crimes receive such different sentences? Wouldn't it be fairer to have set and mandatory sentences to ensure uniformity in the criminal justice system? Although I then saw the great need for such strict uniformity, I now see that there is even a greater value in allowing judges and juries discretion to "make the punishment fit not only the crime but the criminal as well."

Only a few hundred years ago, the theft of a loaf of bread was punishable by death in England, the source of most of our legal heritage. Although such cruel punishment seems absurd and inhuman to our modern minds, in the sixteenth century, it took all the persuasive powers of such great leaders as Sir Thomas More to sway public opinion to a more humane and reasonable approach to criminal justice. In his famous book, *Utopia*, More argued in the year 1517 that the facts and circumstances of a man's life should enter into the equation of what punishment was merited for a particular crime. His principal character stated More's philosophy as follows:

> "It happened one day that I was at his table, and a certain layman was there, learned in your laws. On some pretext or other he began loudly to sing the praises of the stern justice which was then being used in England against thieves, who, he said, were strung up everywhere, sometimes twenty on one gallows. And so he said he was all the more puzzled, when so few escaped punishment, what evil fate produced so many robbers all over the country. Then, presuming to speak freely in front of the Cardinal, I said, 'There is no reason why you should be surprised. For this punishment inflicted upon thieves is beyond the bounds of justice and not to the public advantage. It is too

severe for punishing robbery, but not sufficient to restrain it. For simple theft is not so great a crime as to deserve capital punishment, nor is there any penalty strong enough to keep from theft men who have no other means of gaining a livelihood. So in this matter not only you, but a good part of this world also, seem to copy bad teachers, who more readily beat their students than educate them. For harsh and terrible punishments are inflicted upon thieves, when it would be much better to see that they had a means to earn a living. In this way they would be freed from the awful necessity of stealing and then being put to death."[41]

His words, written for a British society in which poverty was rampant, are equally relevant to our American society today. As of this writing, America is in the midst of a lengthy recession in which 14.2 percent are in poverty. The poverty rate for children is 21.8, a 22 percent increase since the 1980's.[42] Even worse, we may consider our nation to be in a moral recession. Violence and brutality are evident in every day's headline, in most of the movies and T.V. programs and, indeed, in part of our everyday lives. There has been an overwhelming temptation to meet this violence with more violence. Over the past decade, the criminal justice system has been "toughened" to meet this challenge, primarily in the form of both longer sentences and mandatory sentences, which takes away the discretion of the judge once a defendant has pleaded or been found guilty.

Longer mandatory sentences have been particularly enacted for crimes involving illegal drugs. In 1984, Congress passed the Sentencing Reform Act, increasing the sentences for even mere possession of small amounts of drugs and making the sentences mandatory. For example, the punishment for first-time possession of $50.00 worth of certain drugs may be punishable by a minimum of twenty years or even life without parole. Unfortunately, there are many drawbacks to such drastic measures. First, they have not acted as a deterrent to crime. The amount of crime, particularly drug activity, has actually increased since the Sentencing Reform Act was passed. Secondly, since the prison system was not changed to improve the chances for rehabilitation, recidivism has remained at a high of over seventy percent. The net result is that the taxpayers pay an estimated $20,000 to $40,000 a year to keep an offender in prison, more than it would cost to send them to college! Yet, when the criminals get out, they simply go back to a life of crime, the only thing they have been taught.

Thirdly, since federal judges have been stripped of any discretion in sentencing, they no longer have any role in determining an appropriate sentence. Without any authority to distinguish between a callous, unrepentant offender and one who was psychologically unable to extricate himself from a bad situation, the judges are for the most part just clerks who "rubber stamp" the mandatory sentence. This futile role has caused more than one federal judge to protest in disgust, preferring not to be part of such a mechanical and indifferent system.

On December 19, 1992, the *Los Angeles Times* reported the protest of U.S. District Judge J. Spencer Lidos, who reluctantly sentenced a first-time drug offender to ten years in prison.

> "Since the days when amputation of the offending hand was routinely used as the punishment for stealing a loaf of bread, one of the most basic precepts of criminal justice has been that the punishment fit the crime." U.S. District Judge J. Lett said, "This is a principle which as a matter of law I must violate in this case." Under the law, Lett, a Republican, appointed to the federal bench by President Reagan in 1985, had no choice but to sentence Johnny F. Patillo to at least the mandatory minimum of 10 years in federal prison for Patillo's role in trying to ship a package that contained 681 grams of crack cocaine."[43]

The article further pointed out the illogic and inconsistency in that "five grams of crack is enough to warrant a mandatory five year prison sentence, while it takes five hundred grams of powder to qualify for the same punishment...even though crack and powder cocaine are readily convertible into one or the other on a gram-for-gram basis."[44]

The judge further described his dilemma in that, under his understanding of the law, it would make no difference "if the day before making this one slip in an otherwise unblemished life, Johnny Patillo had rescued 15 children from a burning building or had won the Congressional Medal of Honor while defending his country." The judge further criticized the system as causing gross inequities.

> "It is hard to imagine that there is any other nation in which Mike Tyson, a convicted rapist with a long and unsavory history of prior misconduct, could be sentenced by the judge who presided over his trial to a sentence which will make him eligible for parole in a little more than three years," Lett said, "while Johnny Patillo, a first time offender with a spotless prior record, stands to be sentenced by a congress that has never seen him and never judged him to from twelve years, seven months, to fifteen years."
>
> "Such a system," Lett said, "is worse than uncivilized, it is barbaric."[45]

Another federal judge based in San Diego, J. Lawrence Irving, resigned in frustration over the mandatory sentencing laws. Two more senior judges, Jack B. Weinstein and Whitman Knapp, both of New York, have refused, at their peril, to hear any more drug cases to protest the sentencing laws. They have already been threatened with impeachment by members of Congress.

Although mandatory sentences did have the advantage of imposing uniformity in criminal sentencing, it threw the "baby out with the bath water" in taking away the discretionary power of judges. What is now needed is a sentencing structure that imposes different levels of punishment according to guidelines as to the offender's chances for rehabilitation, the criminal intent of the offender, and any mitigating circumstances of the crime.

## THE HUMAN URGE FOR REVENGE

There is nothing more human or normal than wishing revenge against someone who has hurt us. It also is entirely human to feel that someone who hurts us severely, without reason, is evil, especially, as we have seen, if we do not know that person. Even the most loving person's good will is put to the test when they become the actual victim of a crime.

My own idealism and naiveté was abruptly tested shortly after graduating from college. In 1969, my first wife and I joined the Peace Corps, just two weeks after our wedding and graduation. We were both filled with an indomitable spirit of goodwill and a desire to serve in a foreign country. Our first choice for assignment was Africa, and, like many idealistic graduates of the John Kennedy era, we were assigned to do what we could probably do best, teach English. So, for two years, we taught at a secondary school in the Ivory Coast in what used to be French West Africa.

Toward the end of our tour, we decided on a weekend in Abijan, the capital. We had especially been looking forward to such unheard-of luxuries as ice cream, movies and shopping! Late one evening, returning from a movie (Dracula!?), we naively walked across a poorly lighted bridge over a lagoon to reach our hotel. Scarcely had we entered a deserted area on the other side when two men suddenly approached us from behind. With no warning, they were upon us and I instinctively turned and swung the first blow. I saw in horror that they had knives. We could be killed and my wife raped! I howled like a wild animal, swinging my fists wildly, and landed one blow to the man brandishing his knife in my face. Then I saw my wife knocked to the ground by the other attacker. While she struggled to save her purse, I jumped on top of him and knocked him away. The last thing that I saw was the two of them running away across a grassy field into the darkness.

Enraged and hurt, I recall vividly thinking that if I had a gun at that very moment I would have shot both of them as they retreated! We struggled back to our hotel. A Frenchman, seeing my wife's face and dress splattered with blood, remarked in disgust, "And this is what they call 'civilization!'"

We returned to our small town, Dimbokro, badly shaken and suspicious. Since then, I have always looked behind me whenever I'm in a dark or deserted place. The experience certainly taught me to be less naive and trusting.

This ordeal has also often crossed my mind on questions of self defense in a criminal case. How would I feel as a juror asked to determine the guilt of someone who had killed to protect himself. Could I be objective about the outcome? The experience also revealed the great need of victims to be compensated emotionally and financially by the criminal justice system when they have been violently wronged. It has given me a clear insight into the compelling human drive for the death penalty: when we are most deeply hurt, we thirst for the most terrible revenge, an "eye for an eye." Therefore the criminal justice system must place a shield of compassion and understanding between the criminal and the victim, while at the same time assuring that "justice" will be done, so that the victim need not seek revenge. Clearly, then, any punishment system, including the death penalty, must consider this basic need for emotional compensation to victims if our criminal justice system is to fulfill all of its social goals.

## Sentencing To Balance The Needs Of Society And The Needs Of The Criminal

Setting aside the human urge for revenge and the obvious need in many cases to protect us by separating dangerous psychopaths from society, what makes a criminal sentence ethical? Obviously, the one that will promote the most good to the most people in the long run. But what type and length of sentence is that? Since, with rare exceptions, convicted criminals will ultimately return to society, the most ethical sentence will be the one most likely to return the person to society as a law-abiding and productive member. The more serious the offense, the greater the need for rehabilitation of the person. However, a longer prison sentence does not necessarily afford greater rehabilitation; in fact, we have already seen that our present penal system suffers from a recidivism rate of about 75 percent, three out of every four inmates return to prison after committing new crimes.

A totally fresh approach to the criminal justice system is needed: that is to accept that most criminals are simply unloved male youths who grew up in poor to disastrous circumstances. As a criminal trial attorney in the U.S. Navy Judge Advocate General Corps from 1974 to 1980, I came to realize that, inevitably, the young men who committed crimes came from homes beset with violence, alcoholism, abuse and indifference. As a defense attorney, I came to expect a parade of horrors at the point in my legal counseling when I asked my client, "Now tell me about your childhood." In fact, I soon realized that my job as a defense lawyer was 90 percent proving the extenuating and mitigating circumstances of the crime and the defendant and only 10 percent contesting the issue of guilt, since proof of guilt was usually overwhelming.

Before serving as a trial attorney, I was the legal officer on board the *USS MIDWAY* (CV-41) and had the responsibility to prepare all criminal charges for both Captain's Mast and Courts-Martial. Two experiences helped me understand that severe and lengthy punishment is not the only way to ensure discipline. At one Captain's Mast, a sailor accused of a crime became so belligerent and hostile that he actually tried to take a swing at the captain. The sailor screamed out violently and had to be subdued by the master-at-arms. I was aghast that anyone could be so foolish and irrationally violent as to do what he did. At the end of the mast hearings, however, the CO directed me to go to the brig and talk to the sailor to see what was wrong with him. Upon reaching the brig, I saw not the violent man who had just assaulted his commanding officer, but a youth bent over in tears and grief. Between sobs, he asked me to tell the captain he was deeply sorry for what he had just done and he sincerely apologized. He also blurted out that he had just received bad news from home, and the day of his mast was also his birthday. So much for the mean, tough guy thirty minutes before! Of course, I relayed this to the captain, who seemed to have sensed this distress in one of his crew.

Another lesson about crimes and human nature came as a result of the change in command on board my ship. For a year and a half, the *MIDWAY* was skippered by a tough, no nonsense man who personally saw to it that any sailor caught with even a trace of marijuana would get ten days in the ship's brig with no exceptions. He and the chief master-at-arms prided themselves on their efforts to rid the ship of drugs, and, as the new legal officer, I too became caught up with the unswerving policy that any trace of marijuana would automatically land a sailor in the ship's brig. A year later, a new captain took command, and, to everyone's great surprise, announced that, for simple use or possession of marijuana, the punishment would only be restriction to the ship and a fine! We were all dismayed, certain that the ship's discipline would soon disintegrate and our strictly enforced "zero tolerance" for drugs would become a shambles. Much to our surprise, however, the *USS MIDWAY* remained afloat and its combat readiness stayed about the same as before. It was quite an education for me to see that a naval vessel could be run as well on compassion and understanding as it could on strict force and harsh punishments.

I have come to understand that people who commit crimes are, after all, people, and people respond just as well to love as they do to hate and violence, at far less cost and with far greater effect.

Unfortunately, Congress has recently responded to the public outcry for it to "do something" about crime by resorting to the same old policies: more mandatory sentences and tougher penalties. Forty more crimes have been made punishable by death by the 1993 Crime Bill. Only a few senators voted against it, arguing that our society is not going to be improved by further criminalization, more prisons and more courts. The bill did have some excellent provisions, however: more police and more programs for rehabilitation. We need to be able to stop crime before it starts and change offenders instead of hardening them. But the "tougher" sentences and additional death penalty crimes simply will have no substantial effect, as I will explain.

It is extremely politically provident for a politician to appear "tough" on crime, and equally devastating to appear "soft" on crime. Thus, when President Clinton and Governor Wilson of California recently announced a "third strike and you're out" policy, there were few politicians courageous enough to argue against such a rule. At first glance such laws would seem to be just common sense: any person who has committed a third violent crime deserves to be imprisoned for life. Certainly society deserves such protection.

But why limit our sentencing in this fashion? Why should we suppose, for example, that a rapist once convicted, is ever going to change after even his first conviction...unless he has undergone a convincing and total rehabilitation. Rather than arbitrary rules, *any* violent offender should be sentenced to life upon his *first* conviction, until such time as he or she has been convincingly rehabilitated to the unanimous satisfaction of a parole board. Such a flexible approach would keep violent offenders behind bars as long as necessary and would release the rehabilitated, at substantial savings to the taxpayers.

The three strikes law, as recently written in California, is no exception to the "rule" that all strict rules lead to absurdities and disastrous results. Just recently, a man was sentenced to twenty-five years to life for stealing a pizza! Why should the taxpayers subsidize this offender for the rest of his life for such a crime? It would be a lot cheaper just to buy him a lifetime supply of pizzas!

Finally, more and more religious and legal leaders have called for an end to the harsh and mandatory criminal sentencing laws. Reform is particularly needed in the sentencing of drug offenders. A petition proposed by the Coalition of National Drug Policy Change called on society to recognize that drug abuse was a medical and social problem and should be treated with medical and social solutions, not just by harsher and stiffer criminal penalties.

## THE ETHICAL USE OF ULTIMATE FORCE: THE DEATH PENALTY

Let us review the ethical principles applied to criminal sentencing thus far. First, there should be no absolute, fixed sentences: the duration and extent of punishment must vary, given the individual facts and circumstances of both the crime and the background of the person committing the crime. Secondly, the punishment must balance the needs of society and the criminal, that is, practically speaking, it usually must focus on the end effect upon the defendant as that person re-enters society. Appropriate sentencing always must be based on who the person is and why the crime actually was committed, not simplistic labels of "good" versus "evil." Finally, some degree of force is necessary in the imposition of virtually all punishment. Even Mahatma Ghandi's philosophy of nonviolence required its adherents to take such action as resistance to authority, strikes, and physically thwarting the actions of others. Mahatma Ghandi's favorite weapon to ensure his aims was fasting, which was certainly a form of physical violence to himself. It also was an incredibly powerful and morally persuasive force. Inevitably, some degree of physical force is inherent in the imposition of any type of control over others and particularly in criminal punishment. We are not, therefore, questioning whether physical force may be used in the imposition of criminal punishment, but instead what extent of physical force will be appropriate for a given crime.

This simple truth is important as we approach our ultimate criminal law ethical question, the death penalty, because it establishes a framework in which we may view the death penalty question: that is, essentially whether the death penalty is a punishment different from other criminal punishment only in the quantity of force used.

The variety of punishment obviously is as extensive as the variety of crimes. On one extreme, we may have a young teenage mother caught stealing food to bring home to her children. The appropriate "punishment" here may be psychological and vocational counseling during a period of probation. On the other hand, our nation has been witness to heinous and grisly murders executed in unspeakable depravity. Are there crimes so heinous, premeditated and so destructive to human life that only the death penalty could vindicate society?

Since most crimes giving rise to death penalty considerations involve killing, let us note that killing by itself can either be "good or bad" depending on society's approval. When a young man is sent to war in our country, and skillfully and courageously kills hundreds of the enemy, he returns a hero, not a murderer. For example, Congressman Randy "Duke" Cunningham was elected Congressman from California, no doubt in part due to his popularity as the only fighter pilot in Vietnam to become and ace, that is he killed five enemy pilots during that conflict. Even though it is now generally considered that the Vietnam war was a moral and ethical failure, Congressman Cunningham is still considered a hero, not a murderer, because at the time that he did this killing, it was with his country's approval. The point is simply that if in the international context we must look at the purpose and circumstances of the killing to determine if it was ethical or not, certainly we must do the same in the case of a killing committed within our own population.

It was, therefore, an appropriate ethical breakthrough for the United States Supreme Court to do its reversal on the question of the death penalty. When it decided in 1972 in the *Furman v. Georgia* case that the death penalty as imposed was unconstitutional because of the lack of uniformity and lack of guidelines, the court was making an ethical breakthrough. Later, however, in 1976, it held in *Gregg v. Georgia* that the death penalty was not per se cruel and unusual under the Constitution, if it was imposed in accordance with comprehensive guidelines. This was another breakthrough in the ethics of criminal sentencing. As it stands now, the death penalty is constitutional, provided that a state creates strict guidelines for its imposition, so that the death penalty cannot be imposed unless the circumstances of both the crime and the person committing the crime are all considered and fit within certain criteria. The criteria and procedures under the revised Georgia statute were described by Justice Stewart as follows:

> These procedures [established by the Georgia statues] require the jury to consider the circumstances of the crime and the criminal before it recommends sentence. No longer can a Georgia jury do as Furman's jury did: reach a finding of the defendant's guilt and then, without guidance or direction, decide whether he should live or die. Instead, the jury's attention is directed to the specific circumstances of the crime: Was it committed in the course of another capital felony? Was it committed for money? Was it committed upon a peace officer or judicial officer? Was it committed in a particularly heinous way or in a manner that endangered the lives of many persons? In addition,

the jury's attention is focused on the characteristics of the person who committed the crime: Does he have a record of prior convictions for capital offenses? Are there any special facts about this defendant that mitigate against imposing capital punishment (e.g., his youth, the extent of his cooperation with the police, his emotional state at the time of the crime). As a result, while some jury discretion still exists, "the discretion to be exercised is controlled by clear and objective standards so as to produce non-discriminatory application."[46]

I believe, as in the abortion issue, that we must place ultimate trust and faith in the decision maker to determine when the death penalty is ethically required. In the abortion issue, I believe that only the woman herself, empowered with both her knowledge of her circumstances and her innermost feelings, can decide that she can or cannot be a fit mother. Similarly, it is only the criminal law judge or jury who, caught up within the presentation of all the evidence relating to a crime and, most particularly, the defendant's background, psychological state, motivation for committing the crime and potential for future rehabilitation, can actually determine whether the death penalty should be imposed.

As in the abortion issue, this leaves us with no strict, absolute rules and, inevitably, allows the possibility of inequality in sentencing. It also places a terrible burden on judges, juries, prosecutors and defense attorneys to bring forth all the facts and circumstances of the case and to fashion the most appropriate punishment. As in the abortion issue, the very process of the death penalty trial, therefore, will determine whether the death penalty may be ethically imposed in a given case. It could very well happen that two death penalty cases tried in adjoining court rooms with virtually identical criminal allegations will result in the death penalty in one case and not in the other, the only difference being the judge or jury's perception of who the defendant was, what caused him to accomplish the crime and the defendant's future prospects for rehabilitation.

For example, two women may be found guilty of murdering their husbands in cold blood. One did so after a decade of horrific physical and psychological abuse, to the extent that on several occasions the woman feared for her life. In the other case, the woman's primary motivation in murdering her spouse was to obtain a $500,000 life insurance policy. It is easy to see how two murders resulting in identical loss and suffering could result in two extremely different punishments, depending on the circumstances of the crime and the background and motivation of the defendant.

Is there a crime so heinous and destructive that the only appropriate sentence would in fact be the ultimate separation from society, that is the death penalty? On February 26, 1993, six people were killed and over a thousand injured at the World Trade Center in New York City. Four suspects to the crime were found within days, and the motivation for the crime was found to be ideological warfare. All four were Islamic militants willing to advance their cause at any cost of human suffering. One would have though that, if the death penalty ever had a clear case for imposition, this was it. Yet, the four defendants ultimately received only life in prison without parole.

It would be one thing for the defendant or defendants committing such crimes to have done so with the only calculation of achieving some financial or ideological reward. But what if one of the defendants was found by the jury to have been abused as a child, abandoned by his parents and psychologically vulnerable to extortion by fanatics that took him into their fold? Just as with a woman's decision to abort a fetus, I find it impossible to prejudge a defendant given a particular crime. The only people who can really determine an appropriate sentence for a given crime is the judge or jury immersed in the process of determining exactly how the crime occurred and the motivation of the particular defendant. In short, the death penalty is not only constitutional, but it may be ethically required in certain circumstances. However, its imposition should obviously be a rarity, as indeed it is. The continuing and seemingly insurmountable problem with the death penalty is that its imposition is not only a rarity, but it is being imposed so rarely and randomly that its imposition is as much a freak accident as is death by lightning!

## EXECUTION BY LIGHTNING?

The imposition of the death penalty in this country has been compared to ancient ritual sacrifice by Paul Morrow of the Capital Resource Center in Nashville, Tennessee, and the statistics prove this description to be alarmingly accurate.

The number of people facing death row at this point in the nation is only about 2,600, while there were 23,760 prisoners sentenced for murder or non-negligent manslaughter in 1992 alone.[47] This suggests that less than 9 percent of all murder convictions lead to sentence of death. Furthermore, only about 30 of the 2,600 each year are actually ever executed! That means that far less than one out of a thousand convicted murderers is actually executed each year.

However, if a ten-year period of time is considered, the chances of execution are even less; in fact, the chances of execution is only one out of 6,375!

> The chances of a murderer being executed are very, very small. The Bureau of Justice Statistics counted 204,000 reported murders tallied in the FBI's *Uniform Crime Reports* between 1975 and 1984 (the latest year for which complete figures are available). Approximately 198,000 people were arrested for these murders. During this same time period, 2,384 people were sent to prison to be executed for murder. Of this total, 32 were actually executed. A typical killer had a one in 6,375 chance of having to die for his or her crime.[48]

Thus, under the new guidelines for the imposition of the death penalty set by the Supreme Court, the death penalty is being imposed only in the most extraordinary cases, and, undoubtedly, in a totally unpredictable way. For this reason, Supreme Court Justice Harry A. Blackmon recently announced he would vote against all future death sentences, contending that the system "remains fraught with arbitrariness, discrimination, caprice and mistake."[49]

Additionally, our nation pays an extraordinary price for attempting to impose this totally random death sanction. Clearly, we taxpayers are hardly getting any value out of this system. The reality is that we do not have a functioning death penalty in the United States, if less than one out of 6,375 convicted murderers is actually executed each year. Instead, what we have is a full employment opportunity for the lawyers and judges within the criminal justice system. It is extremely common for the appeals for death penalty cases to last ten, eleven, twelve even fourteen years, as with the case of the execution of Robert Harris.

The case of O.J. Simpson is a "teachable moment" concerning the way our nation's criminal justice seeks to administer the death penalty sanction. The prosecutors decided not to seek the death penalty in this case, although the evidence established that he brutally butchered his ex-wife and her friend with a knife. If these vile and reprehensible double murders do not at least invite exposure to the death penalty, what does? Certainly, we cannot carve out an exception to the death penalty that it's OK to murder your spouse or ex-spouse! The Simpson trial highlights the urgent need of our nation to totally refocus the imposition of punishment in our criminal justice system.

Certainly, there is not much deterrent effect created by our present death penalty system, which needs to be totally revised. We need a new system that places less emphasis on trying to label people as evil, and hence meriting the death penalty, and more emphasis on resolving what to do with murderers on a practical basis. I propose that the death penalty should be replaced with an entirely new concept of an ultimate sanction. However, let us first take a more detailed look at the delay, expense, heartache and randomness that is involved in a typical execution in the United States.

## THE EXECUTION OF ROBERT ALTON HARRIS

Call to your mind the image of the person you most cherish and love, perhaps your spouse or child. Now, imagine you have just been informed that your loved one has been brutally and senselessly murdered. You now are somewhat in the frame of mind of the survivors of the victims in probably the most famous death penalty case in recent California history.

In 1978 at the age of 26, Robert Alton Harris murdered two Clairemont Mesa teenagers with executionlike brutality, then used their vehicle to rob a bank. The most notorious part of the entire episode was that, after murdering the two boys, Harris calmly and nonchalantly finished off the cheeseburgers that they had just purchased before they were murdered. The execution-style murders of the two youths sent the Clairemont Mesa community into shock and anguish. However, none of the victims' relatives and loved ones could have suspected that, after the apprehension and conviction of Robert Harris, the nightmare of their grief and sadness would endure for a fourteen-year period of appeals and last-minute stays of Harris's execution.

Why did the survivors' grief and mourning have to drag on for over a decade? Although some of them did not live to see Harris's execution, those who did could not feel vindicated and that the matter was resolved until Harris had died. On the next page is a photograph taken April 22, 1992, showing one of the victim's two brothers sobbing, and wiping away the tears as he was finally informed that Harris had been executed. Clearly, the execution was an emotional catharsis for the relatives of the victims.

However, those who witnessed the execution reported Harris as gesturing to one of the victim's fathers, (who in fact was one of the officers who arrested Harris) and saying to him that he

# Harris Dies After Judical Duel

## 4 Stays Quashed: 'I'm Sorry,' Murderer Says

■ EXECUTION: California invoked the death penalty for the first time in 25 years after a night of delays. The event is videotaped for possible hearings.

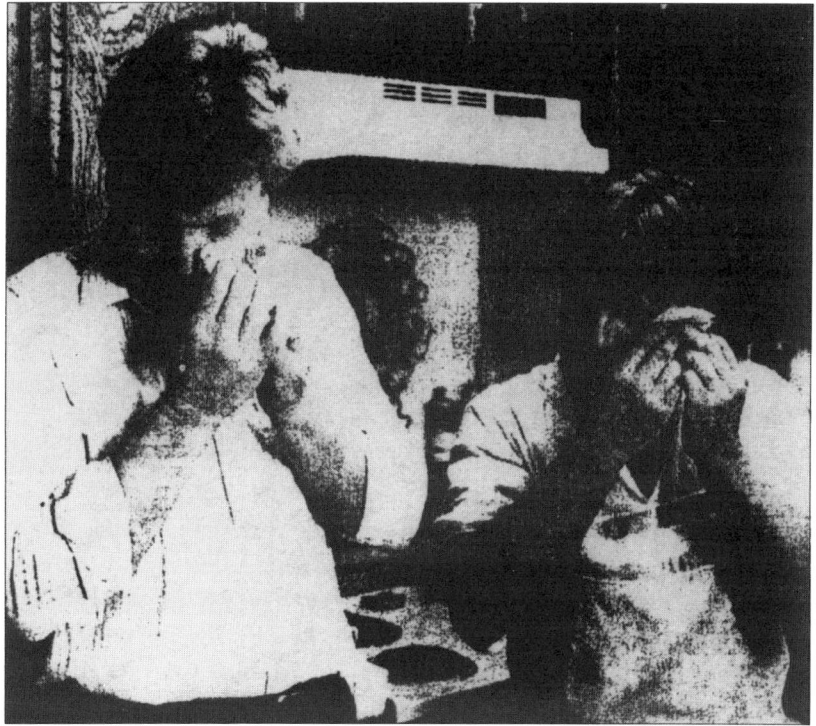

Ed, left, and Anton Mayeski in San Diego after learning that Robert Alton Harris had been put to death. Harris was executed for the murders of their brother, John, and his friend Michael Baker in 1978.

was sorry to have caused such severe pain and suffering to so many people. One of the victims' sisters also described Harris' dignity and remorse during the execution. She reported Harris's conduct as he walked for a second time into the gas chamber, two hours after the U.S. Supreme Court had dissolved the stay that temporarily spared his life.

"The second time, he knew," Clark said. "There was remorse there. You could just see it. No smirky smiles. When he knew it was finally over a totally different man walked into that room.

"Harris sat down in the chair and looked straight at Steve Baker. I think it was the hardest thing he ever did," Clark said. "He really wanted the family members to know he was sorry. He looked right at Steve and said 'I'm Sorry'. You could see he really honestly meant it. It was a special moment.

"I just broke down and cried. I knew what he was trying to tell us and I looked at him and I saw just another human being so I tried to reach out in a way, I cannot explain this very well, a spiritual way, and tell him I could forgive him because he was giving his life like that, accepting it like a man.

"The cyanide gas seemed anything but cruel and unusual," she said. "Even when he was gasping for air, he took big gulps to get it over with. Then he went to sleep, there was no jerking. He rolled, back and forth, like something was bothering him in his dreams.

"When I saw his head go down for the last time, I said a prayer for him," she said. "It was like, I just hope he's taken out of his misery. I felt Harris was at peace with himself for what he had done.

"Then I just totally felt this rush at being at peace with myself. I never thought in my life that

this would come over me. All the hatred inside me totally disappeared. It was like the miracle of forgiveness. Before I couldn't do it. I couldn't forgive him.
And then I did".[50]

It seemed that only Harris's execution could bring an end to this painful chapter in the lives of those affected by this tragedy. As the sister of one of the victims put it,

"I've been suffering for thirteen and a half years," she said. "Harris has been sentenced. He ought to pay. It's time. He should suffer."
She added, "I owe this to Mike. I want to see it for myself, watch Harris die. Once he's gone, I can get on with my own life. Knowing that Mike can rest in peace, the family can get on with their own lives."[51]

Was this revenge the only way out of their pain and grief? There was substantial evidence brought forth at the trial that Robert Harris' childhood had been a living nightmare. As a young boy he was constantly subjected to both physical and emotional abuse by his parents. He also from birth suffered from fetal alcohol poisoning by the alcoholism of his mother. At a time far too late to do him any good, psychological evidence was produced as a basis for an appeal that established that Harris lacked the mental capacity to either tell right from wrong or to refrain from doing wrong, the tests for mental insanity. There was thus substantial evidence on which the jury could have recommended life imprisonment as opposed to the death penalty. I am not suggesting that it is appropriate to second-guess the jury. The jury has the best opportunity to create the proper criminal sentence by witnessing the entirety of the trial. But there was serious question whether this jury received all the information it needed to resolve Harris's fate. This was such a tragic and borderline case that two juries hearing the same facts, but with different lawyers, psychologists and membership of the jury could, in fact, have rendered opposing opinions on the death penalty. That being true, it seems to me that a safeguard is needed to protect against the possibility that an innocent man might be executed or that a guilty person be executed when a lesser form of punishment might have been appropriate. That safeguard lies within the hands of medical and psychological science as we seek to learn more about the human mind and the control of human behavior.

## AN ALTERNATIVE TO THE DEATH PENELTY

> *By no means every conflict of duties, and perhaps not even a single one, is ever really "solved," though it may be argued over, weighed, and counterweighed till doomsday. Sooner or later the decision is simply there, the product, it would seem, of some kind of short-circuit. Practical life cannot be suspended in an everlasting contradiction.*
>
> Carl Jung, *Memories, Dreams, Reflections*

Imposition of the death penalty is one of those "all-or-nothing," "either/or" decisions that, tragically, are limited by both human error and by the imperfections of the trial and jury system. No one is guaranteed a "perfect" trial under the Constitution, and sentencing by a jury of one's peers may well end up with the same results as if one underwent brain surgery by a team of twelve of one's peers. Certainly, one of the worst horrors presented by the death penalty is the possibility of executing an innocent person.

How are we to resolve the ethical dilemma proposed by the death penalty? It is one of those dilemmas that, as Jung would point out, has no resolution. Opponents of the death penalty will never be satisfied until it is removed. Proponents of the death penalty will feel cheated if this ultimate terminating sanction is not available and imposed from time to time. One resolution of this issue is not to decide for or against the death penalty, but instead to create an entirely new concept of an ultimate sanction for criminal behavior. I propose that we replace the death penalty with an ultimate sanction, which would, after conviction for a capital offense, place the criminal's life finally in the hands of a panel of psychologists, psychiatrists and ethical specialists who would determine precisely what would happen to the individual after his conviction. As a protection for society, the court or jury could specify that the most lenient permissible action would be life imprisonment, but the individual could be executed only if he chose not to cooperate with the panel or if he committed another felony while in prison. In any case, I believe that medical science, psychiatry and a new science of ethics will pave the way for a criminal justice system that recognizes the inherent humanity of each and every human being, and the possibility that each person, no matter how depraved, can be, to varying extents, cured of a criminal disposition.

Certainly all such prisoners, no matter what crime they have committed, need both psychological and psychiatric rehabilitation to break their cycle of crime. Equally important would be psychotherapeutic and psychiatric intervention, including administering drugs for those whose chemical imbalance causes their lives to become irrational, unpredictable and antisocial. For incurably violent prisoners, however, life imprisonment would have to be imposed.

The most vital reason for our nation to adopt this alternative to the death penalty is not so much to respect the humanity of the small handful of people on death row; rather, it is to manifest a new American commitment to honor the potential for good in all men and women, to recognize that any one of us, raised in a sufficiently depraved environment can end up in such criminal misery, and, that, under this nation, we are all fundamentally equal. If any one of us, but for the grace of God, could have become a murderer, then none of us should be executed by the state.

Thus, if we turn our focus away from killing the 2,600 on death row and toward the remaining 948,881 felons and to many millions of potential felons, we, as a nation, will be a lot better off.

Another vital reason for adopting such a system lies with the actual causes of crime. We all know that a child born into a world of addiction, abuse and abandonment is more likely to become a criminal. What we don't know, however, are the chemical and genetic components that cause some men to commit heinous crimes. This is the famous nature versus nurture question of how men become criminals. Research, however, has made us see that our dispositions are far more controlled by chemical and hormonal imbalance than we realized. Professor James Wilson has written extensively on this issue. He explains that a physiologically normal person "does not need endless exciting experiences to find happiness; an abnormal person does."

> For example, many scholars have long known that there is some biological basis for criminality, but they have been unable to specify what causes this heritable tendency. Some have thought that criminals are underaroused: that is, they seek excitement because their own psychic state does not supply much, and they find it harder to learn from experience.
> To test this theory, some psychologists examined the level of arousal of about one hundred fifteen-year-old English schoolboys. They did this by measuring their heart rate, how readily their skin conducted electricity, and their brain wave patterns. Nine years later, when the boys were twenty-four, the psychologists looked up their criminal records. Those who had been convicted of a serious crime were much more likely to have had as teenagers a slow heart rate, lower skin conductance, and a distinctive pattern of brain waves. These findings are consistent with the view

that the source of moral sentiments is human sociability: people who are underaroused are less sensitive to the behavior of others and learn less easily from their contact with others.[52]

Professor Wilson also points out that impulsive boys have low levels of the enzyme, monoamine oxidase (MAO), and of a neurotransmitter, serotonin. They, therefore, are under-aroused and are "less sensitive to the behavior of others." Such boys are more likely to become addicts and to have psychiatric problems.[53]

One of the pioneer researchers of the effect of low levels of serotonin is Dr. Markku Linnoila, who has spent thirteen years examining the spinal fluid and blood of more than a thousand Finnish prisoners. His research reveals consistently that violent offenders have low levels of this neurotransmitter and are thus prone to impulsive and violent acts, especially in connection with the use of alcohol. However, often research and work in this field gives rise to the great fear that government will begin programming people's lives. The only response to this must be that providing people with proper medical treatment and chemical balance is far less intrusive than locking them up for lengthy prison sentences or executing them!

An example of one of the recent miracle drugs discovered to cure what used to be called manic-depressive disorder and is now called bi-polar disorder is lithium. This is one of the drugs used to cure the swings of behavior from depression to acting-out in many cases. My personal acquaintance with one of my friends beset with this disease has helped me understand the efficacy of these drugs. As my friend puts it, without that one pill each day, he could not control his life and would inevitably return to the sudden swings of moods that caused him to act out violently in the past. Those criminals who have been suffering from such chemical imbalance certainly must be afforded psychiatric intervention and medical treatment to end their cycle of crime. In any event, proper medical treatment costs much less than prosecutions and imprisonment.

In the case of those convicted of such heinous crimes that this ultimate penalty is imposed, I propose that such individuals be given a final choice in their lives: either submit to the psychiatric intervention that could alter their behavior and chemical makeup, removing their tendencies to violence and acting out, or undergo imposition of the death penalty. This is not to suggest that medical treatment alone can change a criminal disposition; clearly, the prisoner must have the will to change his behavior. And society must find the means to be absolutely protected from any person identified as a danger, whether this be life imprisonment or release with electronic monitors to guarantee that the person will continue medications.

Just as in the abortion issue, the best solution is to provide education to prevent the need for abortions; so, too, the death penalty issue may be circumscribed by identifying the criminally ill and preventing these crimes from happening. The most violent and depraved offenders should be administered psychologic/psychiatric intervention and incarceration for as long as necessary. In that way, society would be protected without resorting to the extreme violence that we deplore in these criminals.

But what of the human need for revenge, for the sense of completion that would come, as in the Harris case, from the final execution of the criminal? This question strikes at the fundamental tenant of Christ's teachings: that we are here to love one another and to forgive each other. Are we to forget this teaching when it comes to our most critical point of justice? I believe that the proper approach for such cases would be the thorough education of the public as to how people come to act in such destructive, antisocial ways. We must understand that, but for a proper and loving upbringing, and a balanced chemical and physiological makeup, "there, but for the grace of God, go I." And for the welfare and advancement of our entire nation, we must remember that, in imposing punishment, the state takes on the role of father. When a father punishes his son, it must always be done with love, to ultimately lift him up, not to strike him down forever.

# The Jury System On Trial:

## The Menendez Brothers

Imagine that you are invited to a major surgical operation and to your amazement, when you enter the operating room you discover that there is not one or two surgeons but eleven surgeons all dressed in white, ready to perform the operation. To your further amazement, you are informed that you will be the twelfth surgeon and, like yourself, the other eleven have been selected at random from off the streets or from a public list of voters.

It is a life-or-death situation, since the patient is seriously ill, and a major surgical procedure must take place. An older supervising physician is seated at a high bench above the operating area. You are advised by the supervising physician concerning basic surgical techniques and the indications for the best procedures, given the symptoms and the condition of the patient. One senior surgeon argues to twelve of you that one procedure is the best to use. Another equally persuasive surgeon tells you that the symptoms call for entirely different type of surgery. Finally, the supervising physician informs you that the twelve of you must all agree. That is, all twelve of you must decide exactly what operation is needed and how it will be done! Imagine how you would feel in such a case! Consider the nightmarish difficulties that would arise as the twelve of you sat down to decide what should be done. Who could doubt the frustration and bewilderment involved in reaching absolute unanimity as you tried to agree on what to do.

Although this is a fanciful scenario, it is painfully similar to the actual task set before the two sets of twelve jurors in the famous trial of the Menendez brothers, tried in Los Angeles for murdering their parents with repeated shotgun fire. Both brothers admitted from the start of the trial the actual killing of their parents. It was therefore left for the jury to decide only the question of their mental state and motivation at the time of the killings. As is often true, the jury took on the role of amateur psychologists and psychiatrists, with the sole task of determining the mental state and criminal motivation of the Menendez boys.

Indeed, they were not only to play amateur psychiatrists, their task was to play the ultimate role of supervising psychiatrists; their unanimous votes would determine which of the parade of psychological and psychiatric experts were the most correct. Their task was then to pigeonhole the psychiatric and psychological evidence into one of the pre-existing legal categories available to them: first and second degree murder, voluntary or involuntary manslaughter.

After six months of testimony and days of deliberation, the juries came back hopelessly deadlocked. Some had found the Menendez brothers to have acted in cold premeditation and held out for first degree murders. Others believed the arguments of the defense that the brothers were victims of long and extensive child abuse and therefore had feared for their lives. They therefore decided on second degree murder or manslaughter. Since no unanimous verdict was reached, the cases would have to be retried. Once again, the prosecution has decided as of this writing to seek the death penalty.

Now let us suppose that a brilliant, passionate and fiery prosecutor succeeds at the second trial where the first prosecutors had failed: he convinces both juries to unanimously agree on first degree murder, thereby setting the stage for the imposition of the death penalty. While that prosecutor's fame will undoubtedly follow him the rest of his life, all it may accomplish will be, under the present system, a series of appeals that could easily last another fourteen years, as in the Robert Harris case. The Menendez boys, even if convicted of first degree murder, will have, like other murderers, less than one chance out of 6,375 of actually being executed. All at an expense to the tax payers of millions of dollars! Again, we have a "teachable moment" in our nation's criminal justice system: just how practical is the death penalty?

However, there is an additional and more profound problem revealed in this scenario. Why do we suppose that a second trial, which reached unanimity, would be more ethically accurate than the first? Why should we suppose that the first trial, which reflected all of the various arguments and psychological realities of the defendants and their crimes, is less accurate or true than a second trial, simply because in the second trial everyone was able to agree? Indeed, would not the first trial, with its varied opinions, more accurately reflect the facts and circumstances of the murders and the mental condition of the boys than a second verdict, where only one version ultimately prevailed?

The Menendez trial, then, is a compelling and teachable example of why we are wasting enormous time, money and psychic energy trying to label people as definitively "evil" and hence candidates for the death penalty. It points dramatically to the compelling need for a system that does not try to reinvent the psychological/psychiatric wheel every time a murder trial takes place. It also points dramatically to our need to do away with the requirement for unanimity on a specific category of murder and instead to charge juries only with the more manageable task of determining beyond a reasonable doubt whether defendants have actually committed a murder. Once they have determined that factual issue, the task of what final punishment to impose upon the defendants should be left to an established team of psychological and psychiatric experts who could monitor the defendants for the rest of their lives.

## O. J. SIMPSON

The murder trial of O. J. Simpson is another compelling example that our criminal justice system seems to be fueled more by money and public sensationalism than reason. By the middle of the trial over $5,000,000 had been spent by the public, even though the prosecution had not even tried to seek the death penalty. Another $3,000,000 was spent before the trial was over. Had there been a conviction, there would have been the inevitable appeals. A comparison with the Robert Harris case, which we have already discussed, and the Menendez Brothers case will virtually speak for itself:

|  | ROBERT HARRIS | O. J. SIMPSON | MENENDEZ BROTHERS |
|---|---|---|---|
| CRIMINAL CHARGE | Brutal murder of two innocent victims | Same | Same |
| PENALTY SOUGHT | Death penalty | Life imprisonment | Death penalty |
| DEFENSE COUNSEL | Public Defender | Probably the most expensive defense team in legal history | Two highly paid lead counselors |
| PUBLIC COST | Minimal cost for public defenders | Over $8,000,000 | Unknown, estimated cost: over a million dollars each |
| RESULT | Two murder convictions/ death penalty | Acquittal | Hung juries |
| APPEAL/ STATUS | Fourteen years to execution | State may not appeal | Retrial on death penalty charges |

A quick comparison of these three cases leads to several regrettable conclusions. First, wealthy men charged with double murders receive a different type of justice than do poor men. Secondly, it appears more permissible to murder your spouse than a stranger!

These cases reveal a fundamental need for change in our criminal justice system. We have to stop the absurdly impossible effort to decide who should be executed in this country. We also have to limit the focus on placing defendants into a criminal category of guilt and place more emphasis on what we do with them once they are determined to be guilty. Elimination of the death penalty as presently administered would take us a long way toward a saner goal of criminal justice!

## THE "HEROIC" DEATH...IS DEAD!

*Some time later God tested Abraham. He said to him, "Abraham!" "Here I am," he replied.*
*Then God said, "Take your son, your only son Isaac, whom you love, and go to the region of Moriah. Sacrifice him there as a burnt offering on one of the mountains I will tell you about."*

*Genesis 22:1-2*

Who were your heroes? Take a moment and write down the names of at least twelve of your favorites. Now, how many of these were assassinated or died tragic or violent deaths? Here are some of my heroes.

| | |
|---|---|
| Jesus Christ | Albert Schweitzer |
| Mahatma Gandhi | Martin Luther King |
| Abraham Lincoln | Carl Jung |
| Thomas Jefferson | Winston Churchill |
| John Kennedy | William Turner |
| Sister Theresa | Joan of Arc |

Note that six of the twelve were assassinated, murdered or crucified. Probably many of your heroes were as well. Little wonder that we seem to think that the supreme devotion is to die for one's cause! Our Western conception of death plays an unfortunate role in both the death penalty and the death-with-dignity questions. Like Abraham, we seem to think that killing a person has a moral significance and value unto itself. By imposing the death penalty, we think we can make "right" a "wrong," as the relatives of Robert Harris' victims clearly felt. Without being consciously aware of it, we are still sacrificing a handful of criminals on the altar of social justice, hoping that such sacrifices will make our society a safer, better place to live. However, we have not yet learned Abraham's lesson, for in the end, God spared him from having to sacrifice his son, and replaced his son with an animal.

Sacrificial death is an ancient concept found in cultures throughout the history of the world. It was most thoroughly researched in Sir James Frazer's famous work, *The Golden Bough*. Greek and Roman mythology is replete with examples of sacrifices. However, a great advance in thinking occurred as human sacrifices were replaced by animal sacrifices. For example, when Agamemnon offended the goddess Artemis, he was required to sacrifice his daughter Iphigenia on the altar of Artemis. As God did with Abraham, however, at the last moment the goddess substituted a living doe for Iphigenia. Unfortunately, we as a nation have yet to learn this lesson—that we do not have to kill our criminally sick members in an effort somehow to hold our society together.

America has fully bought into the historical concept of sacrificial death, without understanding that it can be replaced with a new awareness and value of the living. For us, death has taken on a mystique, mystery and power to the point where it manifests the final meaning and significance for any man's life. We consider death to be the ultimate end for any historical or religious leader. Jesus Christ was born for the very purpose of being killed, we are told. Mahatma Gandhi reached his greatest stature as a world figure upon his assassination. Our own American historical leaders, such as Abraham Lincoln and John Kennedy, reached their highest fame upon their deaths by assassination.

We have tragically come to believe that the best life worth living is one ending in sacrificial death, and that life is not supremely fulfilled unless one has the glorious opportunity of dying for one's cause, whether it be religious or political. This philosophy, when applied in the case of the death penalty, of course justifies dying for one's crimes.

This macho concept has descended even to our artistic world where a totally unrecognized painter such as Vincent van Gogh achieves international acclaim and glory only after his own self-sacrifice by suicide.

The fascination with heroic death is unfortunately only part of the male machoism that has made being a male such a dangerous occupation for many centuries. The men's movement today recognizes that male machoism costs men dearly, both during their lives and in the longevity of their lives. If men are not killed off in a war or in a crime scene, they die nevertheless an average 6.7 years earlier than do women.[54] This shorter life span is at least in part because of the male involvement with power, domination and success, along with the effects of male sex hormones.[55]

Machoism works its way into every part of our society and is clearly found in our approach to criminal justice: where the crime has been sufficiently horrific, the only meaningful atonement is said to be death. But why? Because we have attached such significance to death in the first place! We believe every person's death, and particularly every man's death, is or should be a glorious event that either becomes the ultimate manifestation of the man's life and work such as Christ or Gandhi, or becomes the way by which he atones for his sins. Before we can get away from this super glorification of death, as a nation, we will have to get rid of what might be called "the Old Gringo" syndrome.

In the movie adaption of Carlos Fuentes' novel *Old Gringo*, Gregory Peck plays an aging American author whose only desire seems to be to travel to Mexico to die as part of the glory of the Mexican Revolution. He meets up with General Arroya, one of Pancho Villa's commanding generals and assists him in a battle to take the hacienda where Arroya himself was raised as a peasant. The revolutionaries are victorious, but Arroya falls prey to his own psychological Achilles heel and stays too long at the hacienda, basking in his conquest. Peck sees his moment of glory to be publicly taunting the general for failing to join the larger revolutionary forces. For this, Peck gets his death wish...he is shot and killed by the general. When Arroya is finally induced to leave the hacienda by "Old Gringo's" self-sacrifice, he is aware that he has transgressed the commands of his beloved leader Pancho Villa. He therefore willingly surrenders himself to the Generalissimo, who, before he executes him, gives him a loving and fatherly embrace:

"You know, Thomas, I love you as a son but you must die because you disobeyed orders."

This is male machoism at its "finest" hour! Two useless deaths, all in the name of glory, principle and romantic tradition. Yet, the sad truth is that we are all seduced by the concept of heroic death and, unfortunately, misuse it by concluding that death itself gives us justification for living, not the other way around.

Since, as I believe, the execution of even a vicious murderer would not be as useful to society as his reform, what can be the purpose of the death penalty? Wouldn't the transformation of the convicted person be as wonderful to the victims as the extinction of that person? As the Apostle Paul phrased it, wouldn't the death to the old ways and sins of a criminal be cause for the greatest rejoicing?

Certainly, nothing ever attributed to Jesus Christ suggests that He would believe in an "eye-for-an-eye" death penalty. What He did say was, "If someone strikes you on one cheek turn to him the other also."[56]

The concept of the heroic death is not just a product of male machoism; in addition, it is part of being youthful, naive and idealistic. It is however a naivete which we can ill afford if our society is to progress and mature ethically. In his book, *Once Upon a Midlife,* Dr. Chinen reveals the difference between the treatment of death in children's fairy tales such as the *Wizard of Oz* and the understanding of the reality of death in midlife tales:

> For youth, death is dramatic, heroic, or romantic, and young men and women willingly die for Love, Truth, or Justice. But death is only an abstraction to youth. At midlife, men and women give up this illusion. Death becomes a sobering reality, stark and inevitable, no longer a matter of glory, but of limitation.[57]

If, as Dr. Chinen suggests, ethical maturity requires giving up the notion of the heroic death, we may come to realize how little is accomplished by our erratic and scattered imposition of the death penalty. And if it costs millions of dollars just to execute one man in California, we may begin to wonder if it is worth it. The recent "hung jury" trials of the Menendez brothers are said to have cost three million dollars; yet the clearly divided juries gave little hope that a unanimous verdict of first degree murder would be likely upon retrial. Wouldn't these millions be better spent on the pressing causes for reform and aid within our inner cities?

We should replace the death penalty as it stands, not so much to preserve the lives of a few men and women (thirty a year, approximately!), but as an affirmation of life—a manifestation that we are too busy helping the living to be distracted by our lust for revenge to punish the mentally and criminally ill.

Instead of wasting years of energy in appeals and millions of dollars on a legal structure to establish the ultimate criminal fault of individuals, shouldn't our greater focus be on creating a society where these injuries and wrongs will not occur? Especially since the death penalty system costs a fortune but is worthless as a deterrent to crime.

The truth is that not much will change if the death penalty were to be abolished over night. Remember that there was no death penalty from 1972 to 1976. Furthermore, no one was executed in the entire United States from 1967 to 1977.[58] If the death penalty acts as a deterrent, then the rate of crime should have increased after 1972 and decreased after 1977. However, the rate of murders has actually remained about the same as a percentage of the population since 1973. In 1973, it was 9.4 per 100,000, in 1992 it was 9.3.[59] Furthermore, the rate of crime in non-death penalty states is no higher and is often lower than in states that have capital punishment.[60] And ask yourself if our society is more or less criminally violent than England, Canada, or France, where there has been no death penalty for many years?[61] In fact, the rate of burglary and robbery in England is about the same as in the United States.[62]

In sum, the death penalty is a form of justice that profits us little and costs us a fortune, both in terms of energy and money. It is the ultimate manifestation of violence and brutalization within our society. At last it is time that we replace the death penalty with a system that reflects both the way humans are actually conditioned to behave and the way ethical choices are made. We simply can no longer afford the "heroic death" as part of our criminal justice system. And curiously, we will next see that our notion of the heroic death limits us not only in the way we handle criminal justice, but in the way we resolve ultimately how each and every one of us will die.

# THE SPRING OF 1995:
## THE CONFESSIONS OF MCNAMARA AND THE APPREHENSION OF MCVEIGH

The spring of 1995 was a time of shock, horror and national grieving in America. It was also a time of great emotional unrest and ethical revolution in our nation. It began with the startling public admission and confession by Robert McNamara, the Secretary of Defense under President Lyndon Johnson, that the

Victnam War was a moral mistake and failure. In his book, *In Retrospect: The Tragedy and Lessons Of Vietnam,* McNamara wrote that the war was simply wrong for many reasons. During a television interview he was asked, "How does it make you feel to realize you promoted a war that you now say needlessly cost thousands of American lives?" He replied simply that he did not feel, that feeling was something he never could do...not even with his own family, and not even now as he reflected back on the enormity of this national tragedy.

McNamara, in his own way, thus confessed his role in the killing of over fifty thousand American lives, as well as the innocent women and children lost in the decade long conflict. His long after-the-fact understanding was a brave and dramatic step towards healing the wounds of the nation, and undoubtedly, his own wounds. Yet, no one would suggest that McNamara be prosecuted as a murderer, since these killings were sanctioned by the consensus of the government of the time, even though the end result was, as McNamara admits, the unnecessary deaths of 58,000 American and an estimated three million Vietnamese.

On April 19, 1995, devastation fell upon the heart of the country in Oklahoma City. A massive bomb was exploded at the Alfred P. Murrah Federal Building, taking the lives of almost two hundred innocent men, women and children. The carnage and loss of life was unbelievable...nothing before had prepared us to understand how this could happen in the heartland of our Nation.

Almost instantly foreign terrorists were blamed. The bombing had the "signature" of "Middle Eastern terrorists," we were told. Only they could have perpetrated such a despicable evil. Major newspapers carried the news that Islamic fundamentalists were suspected. People looking Middle Eastern were arrested as far away as London. No one seemed to focus on the obvious fact that the bombing occurred on the second anniversary of the federal government assault on the Waco, Texas compound, which led to the fiery deaths/suicides of over 80 men, women and children.

Less than two hours after the bombing, an Oklahoma state trooper, Charlie Hanger, stopped Timothy McVeigh for speeding and driving without a license plate. He arrested him upon seeing a gun bulge from underneath his jacket. Office Hanger hardly suspected that this young American might be the terrorist who dealt the country so wicked and cowardly a blow. In fact, McVeigh was almost released! Fortunately, his bail review hearing was delayed while the local judge heard a domestic relations case. Then, an FBI agent called to confirm McVeigh's identity and excitedly reported to his colleagues and the world, "they got him, they got him!"

So, once again, we have the met the enemy...and he is among us!

After all the senseless killings, President Clinton responded to this crisis by calling upon the mourning to seek justice. The Government would seek the death penalty for whoever did these cowardly, evil acts. The death penalty? The very words seemed hollow, useless and antiquated. What good would the death penalty do? Of course it would not bring back the dead. And it certainly had failed to act as a deterrent, even through many such crimes were recently made punishable by death by Congressional statute. And it seemed impotent as a punishment given the vastness of the suffering caused by this hideous crime.

The truth is that death...is too good for these criminals. If we really want to punish them, we should imprison them forever, locked up with their own condemnation that they caused more suffering and pain to their countrymen than any one in the history of the nation...unless, of course, you include the suffering caused by the ethical errors of leaders like Robert McNamara.

The lust for revenge is overwhelming in a case like the Oklahoma City tragedy. Yet, at some point and at some time, somebody has to be the one in any conflict to say there has been enough violence and enough killing. If two men are fighting, one has to eventually be the first to stop or give up. If two nations are at war, one has to finally surrender or, as we did in Vietnam, withdraw. And in this cycle of violence in our Nation, someone has to be the first to say, "Enough! The violence must end!"

Unloved, hate-filled and mentally unbalanced men such as Timothy McVeigh will not be the ones to end this violence. We can not expect them to turn our culture around, but we should not allow our culture to revolve around them. In fact, McVeigh may simply have been carrying on in his sick way the violence he was ordered to perform as a soldier in the Persian Gulf War. Reportedly, his military vehicle was one of those used to bury alive hundreds of Iraqi soldiers who were among the thousands overwhelmed by superior forces of the United States and its allies.

If there is to be an end to the killing, it must come from our wise and older leaders, from the aged hearts and minds tempered by realities of long life. It must come from those of us, young and old, who know that, "there but for the Grace of God, go I." It must be, at long last, expressed by our government as the will of the people, sitting as the final father and mother of these sick young people. In the end, it must be the people who call for an end to the killing.

As hard as this may be to accept, killing another young man to add to the hundreds lost in Oklahoma...will heal no wounds. It would not bring back the dead. It may provide the release of revenge, but it would not bring us any closer to a more loving, compassionate society. Such "eye for an eye" justice would only be the crowning manifestation of the nation's ultimate belief in violence as a way of life...and death. Perhaps the time has come, amidst our greatest mourning, to let the spirit of love rise up...and lead us out of our grief and rage.

*Dr. Kevorkian*

# DEATH IN AMERICA

## THE AMERICAN IDEAL DEATH: "KEEP BOTH GUNS BLASTING TILL YOU GO DOWN!"

Our concept of the macho heroic death plays as devastating a role in the question of death with dignity as it does with the death penalty. The majority within our nation are still convinced there is only one right way to die—with both guns blasting till we go down. Compared with the issues of abortion and the death penalty, however, the question of whether one should be able to die a dignified death is comparatively simple. There is no innocent fetus to consider as in the abortion issue and there is no victim to be revenged or society to be protected as in the death penalty issue. Instead, there is simply the individual's decision of whether to prolong a painful terminal illness or to end one's life before the pain, suffering and medical expenses become unbearable. In many ways this, too, is a bogus issue, since anyone who really wishes to take his life is free to do so if he is physically capable. The real issue is—will society tolerate physician-assisted suicide that could be done in a peaceful and dignified manner? One would think that this would be a relatively uncontroversial issue, since each person should be allowed to determine how much pain or how many medical bills they can tolerate prior to the natural ending of his or her life. But in reality, public opinion is squarely divided on this issue.

In 1991, voters in the state of Washington rejected a voter's initiative allowing a physician to assist in the death of a terminally ill person. The issue was narrowly defeated by a 54-to-46 percent margin. In 1992, California voters similarly rejected a death-with-dignity initiative, even though it required two licensed physicians to approve the physician-assisted suicide of a person who had a terminal and painful illness. However, in 1994 Oregon became the first state in the United States to authorize euthanasia.

Why, one may ask, have the majority of voters in every state except Oregon rejected the right for themselves to determine the nature of their own final exit? Again, part of the reason must be our cultural obsession with heroic death and what I have called "the Old Gringo syndrome." We still believe that the manner in which a person dies reflects the ultimate value and worth of his entire life, so that even if a person has led a productive and loving life, he is somehow lacking if he chooses not to endure the final months of his life racked in pain. We still think that this is somehow cowardly and not setting a good example, when in fact the manner by which a person dies really has very little significance compared to the totality of all the things he did or did not do while alive. I don't think a glorious death of conquest over pain would rectify an otherwise meaningless or shallow existence. On the other hand, a fruitful and loving life should not be tainted by choosing to end it several months early to avoid suffering and useless medical bills. Let us look at this issue more closely following the principles that we have used in the previous issues.

## CAN THERE BE AN ABSOLUTE RULE DICTATING HOW WE ALL MUST DIE?

If we tried to create a strict rule concerning how people must die in this country, what would it be? One rule would be to require every possible means of medical and surgical intervention to prolong a person's life, regardless of the quality of that life, the expense incurred by the procedures and the pain that the patient may be enduring. Its opposite rule would be to allow individuals to choose suicide with the help of any physician at any time, simply because they wanted to commit suicide. Either of these two rules would provide the security of knowing exactly what we must do or what we can do in any given medical situation. As with most strict rules, as we have repeatedly seen, they suffer from ignoring all of the myriad differences in human constitution, will power and the infinite variety of medical conditions. Obviously, as with every other strict rule that we have discussed, they would fail to afford the greatest possibility of ethical decisions that truly reflect the mental state and the medical condition of each individual.

Clearly, any absolute rule precluding the manner in which one dies would result in less effective ethical decision making. This is because we are not all alike when it comes to enduring pain and keeping our sanity during devastating illness. Having witnessed my father go through a prolonged year of excruciating pain during a terminal illness and witnessing the tragic personality changes that he underwent because of his disease, I do not wish this to happen to me or to my children. I choose not to force relatives and loved ones to see and endure me in such a condition. I therefore would insist on the right to choose the manner in which my final months on earth take place, just as I insist on the right of other people to determine just how their final days might take place.

I am strongly in favor of a statute that would allow for physician-assisted euthanasia. Note the choice of the word "euthanasia." The difference in connotation between "euthanasia" and "suicide" is the difference between our definition of force versus violence that we described earlier. In the common understanding, suicide is when a person takes one's own life out of psychological frustration, despair or mental illness. Euthanasia, on the other hand, is the taking of one's life when, in a calm, balanced and loving manner, one concludes that it is best for everyone concerned to choose to end one's life gracefully now, rather than after months or years of prolonged agony.

## THE NECESSITY FOR GUIDELINES

As with any ethical issue, competing interests and needs must be respected and balanced in the question of death with dignity. The individual's right of privacy to determine how he will end his life must be balanced against the interest and duty of society to protect individuals from periods of simple depression, the improper influence of relatives or other parties or the improper influence of doctors in determining when and how a person's life must end. Accordingly, the legislature must create a euthanasia statute to accommodate these conflicting rights and interests.

A carefully drafted physician-assisted euthanasia statute would provide for a careful screening out of those cases where people were simply depressed, emotionally imbalanced or in a temporary crisis in their lives, whether that crisis be financial, emotional, or psychological. It should require at least two doctors to concur before the euthanasia would be legally permitted. Furthermore, at least one of the doctors would have to have personally known and treated the patient for at least six months before authorizing the euthanasia. In addition, at least one of the doctors should be a psychologist or psychiatrist familiar with the patient's emotional and mental state of mind. Finally, consistent with their Hippocratic oath, the doctors' first duty would be to find every possible means and form of persuasion to convince the patient that his life was worth living and was meaningful, despite whatever medical, financial and personal hardships he may be undergoing. The doctors would have to document the six-month period of counseling before they gave their authorization for the euthanasia.

Such a legislative program is in stark contrast to the flamboyant, dramatic and off-the-wall assisted suicides by Dr. Kevorkian. As reported in the excellent book, *Final Passages*, by

Judith Ahronheim and Doron Weber, Dr. Kevorkian assisted in the suicide of one woman, Mrs. Adkins, without any patient/doctor relationship and merely by accepting the medical diagnosis made by others.[63] The authors are highly critical of the dominating personal agenda of Dr. Kevorkian and his willingness to assist Mrs. Adkins in her death, having only met Mrs. Adkins once at dinner the previous night before agreeing to assist in her death. The authors further condemned Dr. Kevorkian, since Mrs. Adkins, had played tennis with her son a week before her death and was in good physical health. Certainly this could not occur under the euthanasia statute I am proposing.

As of this writing, Dr. Kevorkian has assisted in *over twenty* suicides and has once faced trial under the Michigan law that makes assisting suicide a felony. His methods may be doing more harm to his cause than good, although he is at least forcing people to think about the issue. He undoubtedly deserves the criticism that he is likely to give merely depressed people the option for suicide. During his recent incarceration, he started a hunger strike, but was ultimately released on bail. Dr. Charles Krauthammer, describing him as a "medical exhibitionist," suggests that his next hunger strike would be "one physician-assisted suicide I would be loath to interrupt!"[64] Yet Dr. Kevorkian's radicalism is no reason to reach the conclusion on the other extreme: that the terminally ill should never have any say about the ending of their lives.

Dr. Kevorkian's picture reminds me of the young beauty/old hag drawing we already examined. Some will see him as a dark agent of Death, the anathema to all that the medical profession holds sacred. Others will see him as the George Washington of final and ultimate freedom in the United States—the revolutionary who sacrificed himself to free us from the bonds of Old World mentality about death. Paradoxically, he is both, just as the drawing of the woman contained both images. Yet, like the drawing, he may be the catalyst to propel us forward to a new way of thinking about death: a grudging, inevitable acceptance that death, after all, is as natural and inevitable a choice within our lives as any other phase of our being.

Holland is the only country where physician-assisted euthanasia is openly practiced. The guidelines require that the patient must be suffering intolerably with no chance of improvement, that the patient requests aid in dying over a reasonable period of time and that the patient is mentally competent to make such a decision. Finally, two physicians, one of whom has not been involved in the patient's care, must agree on the use of euthanasia. I am proposing that we adopt such a system in the United States. We need a legal structure that charts a safe and reasonable course between two intolerable situations: prolonged, needless suffering versus unnecessary suicides. I agree with Ahronheim and Weber, that the key ingredient to such a legal structure is hope, in the sense of worthfulness of the terminally ill. The terminally ill must at all times be valued and supported in their medical and psychological needs. However, that hopefulness must allow for choice in the ethical journey as one nears the end of his life. There must be hope that, through the proper medical care and treatment, a person's final days and weeks on earth may be painless, coherent and loving, so that the person will both be able to receive the love and care of others and be in a position to return some love, guidance and example to their friends and loved ones. But there must also be the hope that, when medicine and medical treatment reaches the end of its efficacy, a person will have the final control over his destiny and may choose the manner and time of his departure from this life. We should, afterall, have some choice as to when we say our final "good-bye."

## The Individual, Not The State, Should Determine The Terms Of Our Deaths

A life filled with love is one where we can not only receive love, but share it as well. During the final days of a terminal illness, however, our capacity to give love may be reduced to nothing, as we become helplessly dependent on machines and medical staff simply to keep us alive. And the pain of a terminal illness may make life impossible to endure without powerful drugs. How can we be in a position to be giving to others in such a helpless state? Shouldn't there be a dignified alternative to such a plight?

One of the reasons given against a euthanasia statute is that there are powerful pain killing drugs that are available to relieve the pain of a person in a terminal illness. These drugs include the powerful narcotic drugs used for severe pain, including morphine, methadone and codeine. All of these drugs are illegal without prescription from a licensed physician. Ironically, we may not choose to use these drugs on our own, but when faced with a terminal illness, as the law stands now we have no choice but to use them! We must truly question the ethical validity of a culture that outlaws painkillers during the course of our normal lives, then makes us dependent on them when we face a painful terminal illness!

If a human being is in such pain and misery that he can only be assisted by massive narcotic drugs, he really can't be said to have a meaningful quality of life. A life extended through massive drug therapy can only create a burden to friends and loved ones. Certainly, one should be able to choose to end one's life if one is truly incapable of being any good to anyone else. If one is rendered incoherent or mentally dysfunctional because of drugs, how can life be enjoyed, and how should people witness the disintegration of one they love?

On the other hand, there should be no criticism of those who choose to continue a terminal illness to its final conclusion by the use of such powerful narcotics as morphine. Dr. Ahronhein has described in detail how accurate and increasing doses of morphine can be administered to a patient until he or she feels comfortable, without necessarily turning the patient into an addict. Certainly, no one needs to turn to physician-assisted suicide because of a fear they will die in pain. However, the terminally ill also need not feel that they must turn to narcotics from fear that they will die in pain. In short, it should be up to the individual how he or she wishes to end his or her life: avoid the pain, disability and incoherence of a terminal illness either by use of massive narcotics, or end one's life at a time that one chooses. The critical point is that the choice should be made in writing by each of us when we are of sound mind and can make the decision free of depression, pain and anxiety. In summation, we must decide the manner in which we wish to end our life; otherwise, it may be decided for us.

## THERE IS NO GOOD OR BAD WAY TO DIE

Obviously, the California death-with-dignity initiative failed to pass in part because there is a cultural belief that the only *good* way to die is to hold on until the end, keeping a "stiff upper lip," pretending to smile even if one really wants to grimace with excruciating pain. However, if a woman has a constitutional and moral right to terminate the existence of a fetus, certainly each individual has a right to terminate his own existence to avoid unendurable pain and suffering during a terminal illness.

We must progress beyond the macho culture that says that enduring pain is a noble and worthwhile cause. The only valid purpose I can imagine for enduring pain is to get through to the other side of it, that is, to reach the end of the illness. Therefore, in the death-with-dignity statute, physician-assisted suicide is permitted only upon certification by two physicians that the illness is terminal, without any possibility of recovery. What can be the possible argument for continuing one's life if its only prospect is ever-increasing pain and misery? Answer: perhaps the fear of death and the fear of what may follow. As Hamlet said,

> *Who would these fardels bear,*
> *To grunt and sweat under a weary life,*
> *But that the dread of something after death—*
> *The undiscover'd country, from whose bourn*
> *No traveller returns—puzzles the will,*
> *And makes us rather bare those ills we have*
> *Than fly to others that we know not of?*
> *Thus conscience does make cowards of us all;*

> *And thus the native hue of resolution*
> *Is sicklied o'er with the pale cast of thought,*
> *And enterprises of great pith and moment,*
> *With this regard, their currents turn away*
> *And lose the name of action.*
>
> William Shakespeare, *Hamlet*

There simply is no valid reason not to allow those who do not fear death, but who do not enjoy terminal pain, to choose to end their lives in the way, time and manner which they choose, not when the disease chooses. In this sense, we should be allowed to approach our death with some peace of mind, as Bryant wrote:

> So live that when thy summons comes to join
> The innumerable caravan that moves
> To that mysterious realm, where each shall take
> His chamber in the silent halls of death,
> Thou go not, like the quarry-slave at night,
> Scourged to his dungeon, but, sustained and soothed
> By an unfaltering trust, approach thy grave
> Like one who wraps the drapery of his couch
> About him, and lies down to pleasant dreams.
>
> William Cullen Bryant

As in our previous issues of abortion and the death penalty, in a very profound and real sense, the individual faced with a terminal and painful illness himself makes his decision valid about whether to end his life by the very process of weighing the alternatives and choosing what seems to be the most loving, caring decision. This decision is obviously made not only on the basis of one's own feelings, strengths and fears, but on the desire not to impose a financial or emotional burden on loved ones and relatives. Just as the woman's decision concerning the fate of her fetus and the jury's decision concerning the fate of a murderer both become "right" because they, in essence, create the decision, so too does the person facing death render his or her decision right by the very process of making the decision.

I am not saying that whatever a person says is "right" is right. Such an extreme relativistic position is, as I have argued earlier, as untenable as the position that hard-and-fast rules must be adhered to by each and every person, regardless of his or her circumstances and conditions. I am saying that in these issues, and most clearly in the issue of death with dignity, the decision of a thoughtful, caring and loving person who is of sound mind and who has given ample time to reflect on the matter will be the ethical decision. It is up to each individual to make his journey of discovery to find and create the appropriate answer for his life and his condition.

Although euthanasia is still illegal in 49 of the 50 states, a significant step toward recognizing the right to determine one's death was made by the Federal Patient Self-Determination Act. This December 1, 1991, law requires every hospital to advise patients that they may direct whether or not they wish life-supporting equipment to be used to prolong their lives if they fall into a permanently unconscious, vegetative state. However, many health care facilities are not giving the advice as required. Nevertheless, the debate has begun, and, in the end, I believe euthanasia will become legal. It is only a matter of time before we give ourselves the freedom not to have the manner of the end of our lives dictated by government and rules.

## FORCE AS PART OF OUR FINAL ACTION

We have found that some degree of force is an inevitable component of both ethical decision making and ethical principles. The death-with-dignity issue is no exception. First, the decision and the authorization for physician-assisted euthanasia shall be at minimum a six-month process of interaction with one's physician and psychologist or psychiatrist, and, indeed, as I envisioned the statute, a real challenge to convince the doctors of the validity of one's request. Remember that the doctors will be charged first and foremost with the goal of assisting the patient to find hope and meaning to continue his life, not the contrary. Only when the physicians can document a six-month period of reasoned decision and a reasoned approach to ending one's life can they give this authorization. Just as one has to "fight" to live, so will one have to forcefully "fight" to secure the right to die under such a statute. There will, therefore, be an element of forcefulness required simply to obtain the authorization for a physician-assisted euthanasia.

Secondly, obviously some minimal amount of forceful action will be required to perform the euthanasia. This may be the simple administering of a lethal pill or an injection, but, nevertheless, it will be a forceful act undertaken in most cases by the patient himself. Normally, it would be as simple an act as that of Dr. Timothy Quill, a New York physician who assisted his long-term patient to take her life by simply prescribing a lethal dose of barbiturates. Both the decision and the very act of the euthanasia will require some minimal element of force.

I make this simplistic point, because it seems that one of the most powerful arguments used against euthanasia is that it does require some forceful taking of one's own life. Yet, as we have come to understand, force is an inevitable part of any ethical decision. It certainly plays a fundamental role of any medical decision, whether the question be to administer drugs, operate on a patient, or forbid a patient to do or not to do certain things. Once we have truly accepted the reality that force is a part of our every ethical decision, then the idea of using force, however minimal, to choose when and how to end one's life, will not seem as strange. Indeed, a hundred years from now, I believe it will seem as strange to people that our era did not allow freedom to choose to end one's life as it does now seem strange to us that people were not allowed to freely choose their own religion hundreds of years ago.

Euthanasia has the further salutary effect that men and women will not have to resort to crude forms of violence to end a life of pain. Recently, John Sinderholm was convicted of voluntary manslaughter for murdering his 68-year old terminally ill wife of 47 years. For many years she had struggled with an incurable brain infection that had totally debilitated her. Her husband, therefore, took it upon himself to shoot her in the head. He then shot himself in the face, but lived to be sentenced by the judge to probation volunteer work. Both lawyers admitted he acted out of "love, concern and commitment."[65]

Another husband who killed his terminally ill wife did not fare so well with the criminal justice system. Roswell Gilbert was convicted of first degree murder for killing his wife who had two terminal illnesses, Alzheimer's and osteoporosis.[66] In another case, a 66-year old woman attempted suicide by first dousing her sleeping husband with boiling water and then setting herself on fire. Both were severely burned. She was described as "weak, depressed and afraid of dying."[67]

Surely, such resort to brutal force to end the life of a terminally ill loved one is pathetic. But it shows the great human need to end the suffering of either ones' self or one we love. A properly drafted statute would provide both a legal and moral means to make the end of one's life as loving and good as the rest of it. There is an obvious parallel here with the abortion issue. Just as the right to abortion has precluded the need for dangerous "at home" abortions, so do we need a euthanasia statute that will preclude people from desperate attempts to end their loved one's suffering. Instead, they will be brought in contact with physicians at such a critical time.

Compare these pathetic "euthanasia" attempts with that accomplished for his wife by the president of the Hemlock Society, Derek Humphrey:

> People often ask me how I came into this rather unusual movement and how I've lasted twelve years. I had no knowledge or interest in euthanasia until one day my first wife, Jean, asked me to help her die. She was suffering from breast cancer that

had metastasized into her bones. She and I both knew her death was only a matter of time.

I saw the logic of her request and agreed to secure a lethal potion of drugs with which she could end her life at a time chosen by her. She was insistent that she would pick the time; in fact, she had a remission and hung on for a further nine months.

But in March 1975, when she was critically ill and very debilitated, her doctors gently informed her that there was nothing left they could do. Jean discharged herself from the hospital, and three days later asked me for the drugs. After we had spent several hours saying our last good-byes, she drank a cup of coffee containing the drugs—which a sympathetic doctor illicitly had supplied—and died peacefully.[68]

What Derek and Jean Humphrey bravely accomplished is something we all should be free to choose, without threat of prosecution. It is only our collective fear of death that keeps us from embracing it nobly and in a civilized way.

## IS THE RIGHT TO DIE GUARANTEED BY THE CONSTITUTION?

Does the United States Constitution establish a right to a dignified death? As interpreted so far by the Supreme Court, the answer to this is a very clear cut "yes" and "no!" The answer is simultaneously both yes and no because for many years the court has upheld so called "passive" euthanasia, while at the same time no court has ever upheld a right to "active" euthanasia. By "passive" euthanasia, we generally mean taking steps to end a person's life by simply withholding a medical service, such as disconnecting a respirator. "Active" euthanasia, on the other hand, involves taking an affirmative step such as injection of a lethal poison into a patient. Except for Oregon, in all states of the United States and in all countries throughout the world, including Holland, it is still a crime to actively assist a patient in suicide. Consequently, doctors have always acted at their peril when they have crossed the line to assist their patients in suicide. Some doctors have been able to escape prosecution for assisting in suicide, others have not. One fortunate doctor was Dr. Timothy Quill, who helped his long-term leukemia patient end her life by prescribing a fatal dose of barbiturates. Dr. Quill went so far as to even write about his experience in the *New England Journal of Medicine;* however, the New York State Grand Jury refused to indict him. On the other hand, we have already discussed the infamous Dr. Kevorkian who has faced criminal charges in the State of Michigan.

This state of the law is both chaotic and unpredictable. It is ultimately based on a meaningless distinction between the terms "active" and "passive." Although numerous commentators and authorities have vehemently argued the importance of the distinction and the fine line that is ultimately drawn between the two concepts, I fail to see either how this line can effectively be drawn or why it should be drawn. The main argument is about causation. When a so-called passive euthanasia is accomplished, the cause of the resulting death is considered to be the patient's illness. However, when so-called active euthanasia is performed, the cause of the death is considered to be the doctor's affirmative action. Yet, in both instances, actions are taken by doctors with terminally ill patients with specific diseases who die after the action is taken. In general, the state of the law now is that a doctor may withhold an injection necessary to sustain a patient's life, but he may not affirmatively inject a patient with a substance that would have only the effect of ending the patient's life before the disease caused the patient's death. In summation, our fear of death and fear of abuse or coercion by others gives doctors the final say so in when our lives will end.

It is only a matter of time before active euthanasia becomes as acceptable, understandable and legal as passive euthanasia. Most people today would strongly agree that a person should not be forced to continue on a life support system such as a respirator against his will. At least 36 states have laws granting adults the right to provide advance written directives instructing their physicians to withhold life-sustaining procedures in the event of a terminal condition.[69] And we have already mentioned that federal law requires that every patient admitted to a hospital receiving federal funds must be advised of the right to sign an advance directive indicating whether the person would wish to forgo extraordinary life-saving measures.

However, such enlightened thinking regarding the treatment of the terminally ill has arrived only recently in our legal history. For example, when Karen Ann Quinlan suffered permanent brain damage in 1975, it took a two-year legal battle for her parents to win the right to disconnect their daughter from a respirator. In that case, the New Jersey State Supreme Court found that "the State's right to protect life weakens and the right to privacy strengthens as the prognosis dims."[70]

An equally heart-breaking case was that of Nancy Beth Cruzan, who also suffered severe brain damage in a car accident in 1983. Her parents had to take their case all the way to the United States Supreme Court and then re-open the case back in the Missouri State Court before they were finally allowed to remove the feeding tube that had maintained the life of their daughter. Consequently, in December 1990, the Missouri Court reversed the decision when new evidence of Nancy Cruzan's wishes came to light.[71] Although a state may require clear and convincing evidence of a person's right to refuse medical treatment, the Cruzan decision clearly establishes that a person may refuse medical treatment either directly or through a written directive, even though this may lead to the patient's death.

In the present state of law then, we are entitled to order our doctors not to provide life sustaining treatments, that will ultimately lead to our death, but we may not request our doctor to give us a lethal injection that would determine the exact time that we would die during a terminal illness. Why should the right to choose the manner of our death during a terminal illness not be guaranteed under our Constitution? In every other aspect of life, the Constitution seems to provide power and control over death. In the beginning of life, under *Roe v. Wade*, women have had the right to terminate the existence of a fetus since 1973.[72] And the right to execute persons for criminal activity had been established since the framing of the Constitution. In fact, the death penalty is specifically mentioned in the Constitution.[73] Why then, if women can terminate the existence of a fetus, and society can terminate the existence of convicted criminals, are we not allowed to choose the time and manner of our own death? Certainly the right of privacy found within the Constitution and developed in *Roe v. Wade* should logically extend to the ultimate question of privacy: how and when one dies.

One of the main arguments against extending the right to a dignified death is that it may be abused. That is, elderly people might be psychologically coerced into choosing euthanasia at the request of greedy relatives who do not wish to endure either further discomfort or further financial loss. Certainly these are legitimate concerns and should be investigated; however, the fear of error does not prevent us from constitutionally imposing the death penalty on convicted criminals or from terminating a fetus. Why should there be no protected right to choose the end of one's own life when we have already given ourselves socially the right to choose the end of other people's lives (murderers) or potential lives (fetuses)? Ultimately, whether the right to die is established by statute or through judicial extension of the constitutional right of privacy, our nation has reached the point where individuals should be empowered to determine the ending of their lives. We are finally realizing that, for many of us, our death will be as natural and important a decision as any other choice that we make in our lives.

# Conclusion:
# The Rewards Of Ethical Mysticism— Control, Toleration And Freedom

*I am your life, but if you will not name me, seal up your soul with tears, and do not blame me.*

Inscription on a Norman Crucifix found in 1632

There is both danger and beauty in distilling the essence of one's philosophy. The danger is that the summation of all of one's thinking and theorizing into one set of words or principles provides for virtually no explicit directive on how to conduct one's life. At the same time, inevitably, the summation leaves itself open to unlimited misinterpretation. On the other hand, the beauty is that it serves and fulfills our human craving and need to "name" our philosophy, that is, to reduce it to a word or phrase.

One name that I would give this ethical evolution, distilling it to a single word, would be "control." In the issue of abortion, it is the power of women to control the direction and ultimate responsibilities of their own lives, while at the same time allowing society to control what would otherwise be the unlimited discretion of the woman to determine the existence of the fetus.

In the issue of criminal justice, and particularly the death penalty, society is given the ultimate control over each individual's criminal conduct, while at the same time affording each individual the ultimate decision whether to continue his criminal existence or whether to undergo psychiatric intervention to restore him to a healthy state.

Finally, individuals would be given ultimate control over the time and manner by which their lives end, while at the same time preserving society's responsibility and control over people who might be taken advantage of or who might fall prey to a temporary depression.

In each case, the price that society pays for such ultimate control by and over individual human lives is the loss of the false security that comes from imposing strict rules without exceptions. Our nation must inevitably advance to the understanding that there is a fluidity, indeterminacy and particularity to the realm of ethics. One individual's ethical conclusion in a given set of facts may be and often is as valid as another person's faced with the same circumstances. Again, this is not to argue that all principles must be thrown out and that whatever any one thinks is "OK" is OK. It is not ethically true that "there is nothing either good or bad, but thinking makes it so," but we must understand that strict rules of conduct and rigid laws are likewise not infallible. We have only to recall the United States Supreme Court Dred Scott decision that upheld in 1856 the institution of slavery to realize that, not only are rules made to be broken, but rigid rules strictly applied inevitably produce unethical results. Perhaps this is just another way of calling out for more tolerance and acceptance of each other's ethical views at a time when such tolerance is sorely lacking. During the drafting of this book, two physicians have been senselessly murdered for their participation in abortion clinics. Two more abortion clinic employees have also been tragically killed. A handful of men and women have been executed for no clear reasons to distinguish them from the thousands of convicted murderers who have not been executed. And almost no one has been allowed to choose a peaceful, dignified death at the end of a terminal illness.

Yet, within these ethical issues that we have covered, I have sensed a great need for our nation to come together, bind up its ethical wounds, and grant individuals greater dignity and control over their lives.

A wonderful byproduct of this individual control will be toleration. I say byproduct, because I feel that the best way to reach the toleration so desperately needed in this country is not to seek it directly, but to achieve it upon reaching a truer understanding of what ethical decision making is in the first place. Achieving toleration, then, is like reaching happiness. Happiness comes from fulfilling the goals that have meaning in our lives. Toleration comes from understanding how ethical decisions are reached in our lives. The key to peace in our nation is, then, first and foremost a greater understanding of what it means to be ethical and to act ethically. This understanding is the path we must take to heal our country.

A final name for this ethical evolution is freedom. As I have said throughout this book, we all have grown up in a world and a culture obsessed by fear and guilt. As children, we were constantly told that there was "evil" out there, that life was inevitably difficult, that we were ultimately responsible both for everything in our lives and everything that happened to us. And that war, evil and crime were inevitable.

Most significantly we have been told that, in most crucial things, we just did not have a choice. We all have been burdened with a set of ethical dictates crushing our spirits and individual lives.

So let us end our journey together by leaving behind these ethical burdens we need no longer carry. The good news is that we as individuals and as a society do not have to bring into existence every fetus ever conceived. We do not have to squander billions of dollars and untold energy on a justice system that executes by random ritual sacrifice.

And we do not have to spend the last few months of our lives, debilitated and humiliated, hooked up to expensive machines only to die apart from our friends and love ones. At last, we can be a free people, loving and tolerating each other. At last, we are free to heal the wounds that divide us!

# Addendum:
# Legislative Blueprint For The Future

I have intended this to be a very practical and down-to-earth book. In all areas, I have come down on the side of maximum choice, greatest discretion and maximum control. All of these areas of ethical debate call for clear and powerful legislative reform to guarantee individuals their complete freedom to live, procreate, protect themselves and ultimately to die as they choose. Here is a summary of the legislative implications of this approach to ethics.

## Abortion

1. Freedom of choice should be made either a federal statutory or a constitutional right.
2. RU486 should be legalized.

## Criminal Justice

1. There should be more indeterminate sentencing to allow judges and parole boards the discretion and power to release nonviolent and reformed persons and to maintain as long as necessary violent offenders.
2. Crimes without victims, such as drug offenses, should not have fixed sentences; again, discretion should be given to the judge and parole board to fashion a sentence directly commensurate with the crime. This would have the additional benefit of providing more prison spaces for violent offenders without increasing taxes.

3. The death penalty should be replaced with "an ultimate sanction," which would include a possibility of imposition of death only if the prisoner refuses to submit to psychiatric and psychological intervention and rehabilitation. At the same time, the delay and availability of appeals should be diminished since no one would be executed against his will, except for a felon who commits a murder in prison.
4. In general, sentencing should be done by judges, not by juries. Juries should determine if the ultimate sanction of death is warranted; however, the ultimate determination of what happens in a death penalty case should be made by a sentencing panel.

## Death With Dignity

1. A euthanasia statute should be passed with absolute guarantees to ensure that there is no abuse, either by relatives or by those who are simply emotionally depressed. These guarantees would include at minimum the following:

    a. Two doctors must concur before the euthanasia could be permitted.

    b. One of the doctors must have personally known or treated the patient for at least six months before authorizing the euthanasia.

    c. At least one of the doctors should be a psychiatrist familiar with the patient's emotional and mental state of mind.

    d. Both doctors must first find every possible means to convince the patient that his life is worth living and is meaningful before prescribing the euthanasia.

    e. Both doctors must also document the six-month period of counseling before giving their authorization for the euthanasia.

These are legislative advances for the future, based on the knowledge that we have today. Our information about our own minds, bodies and the environment that we live in is leading us to greater and greater understanding of our human condition and our directions for the future. Just as my own thinking has evolved dramatically over the past two decades, a decade from now I may have entirely new insights, leading me to change my views and evolve my ethical thinking. Yet we will not be able to reach higher points of ethical thinking unless we act on the revelations that have been provided to us in the present. Let us go forth then, prepared to change and, at the same time, be unafraid to change again.

# REFERENCES

## PART ONE: THE MYSTERY OF ETHICAL DECISION

1. The estimate of deaths for the American Civil War is 359,528 Federal troops, and 258,000 Confederate soldiers, for a total of 617,528. *The New Encyclopedia Britannica,* 15th Ed., Vol. 29, p. 237; The numbers killed in our other wars were far less, even when combined: WWI (53,000), WWII (292,000), Korean conflict (34,000) and Vietnam (47,000). U.S. Bureau of The Census, *Statistical Abstract of the United States, 1993,* 113th ed., 1993, Table 564.
2. NAACP Legal Defense and Education Fund; Bureau of Justice Statistics; *Executions* and *Death Penalty.*
3. Ernest Van den Haag, "Why Capital Punishment," symposium on the death penalty, *Albany Law Review,* No. 3-4, (1989-90), 54
4. Attributed to Neils Bohr.

## PART TWO: THE SEVEN MYSTERIES OF ETHICAL DECISION

5. Albert Schweitzer, *Out of My Life and Thought* (New York: Holt, Rinehart and Winston,1949), 155-159.
6. *Los Angeles Times* (hereafter *LA Times*) 30 July 1994.
7. C.G. Jung, *Memories, Dreams, Reflections,* (New York: Random House, 1965), 117.
8. Stephen W. Hawking, *A Brief History of Time,* (Toronto: Bantam Books, 1988), 55.
9. *LA Times,* 16 February 1993.
10. Ibid.
11. Robert Bly, *A Little Book on the Human Shadow,* (San Francisco: Harper, 1988), 36.
12. *Furman* v. *Georgia.* 408 U.S. 238 (U.S. Sup. Ct. 1972).
13. *Gregg* v. *Georgia.* 428 U.S. 153 (U.S. Sup. Ct. 1976).
14. Federal Bureau of Investigation. *1992 Uniform Crime Reports,* 1992.
15. M. Scott Peck, M.D., *People of the Lie,* (NewYork: Simon & Schuster, 1983), 129.
16. Ibid., 128.
17. Ibid., 126.
18. Ibid., 173.
19. *Great Dialogues of Plato,* (New York: The New American Library of World Literature, 1956), 152.
20. Allan B. Chinen, *Once Upon a Midlife,* (New York: The Putnam Publishing Group, 1992), 143-144.
21. Ibid., 148.

22. *Webster's New World Dictionary,* (New York: The World Publishing Co., 1968).
23. Ibid.
24. *LA Times,* 27 February 1994.

## PART THREE: THE SEVEN MYSTERIES AND THE ETHICAL DILEMMAS

25. United States Public Health Service, Division of Reproductive Health, Centers for Disease Control, Atlanta, Georgia.
26. *The Jackson Sun,* 28 November 1993. As of this publication, Wayne Lee Bates has changed his mind and allowed his appeals to proceed.
27. Ibid.
28. LA Times. 9 September 1993.
29. James Q. Wilson, *The Moral Sense,* (New York: The Free Press, 1993), 179.
30. Ginette Paris, *The Sacrament of Abortion,* (Dallas: Spring Publications), 55-56.
31. *Planned Parenthood* v. *Casey,* 112 S. Ct. 2791, (US Sup Ct. 1992).
32. Ginette Paris, op. cit., 62.
33. *Roe* v. *Wade,* 410 U.S. 113 (U.S. Sup. Ct. 1973).
34. Ibid.
35. *Planned Parenthood* v. *Casey,* op. cit.
36. Ibid.
37. Bureau of Justice Statistics, *Profile of Jail Inmates,* 1989.
38. U.S. Department of Justice, Bureau of Justice Statistics, 31 December 1993.
39. U.S. Department of Justice, *Uniform Crime Reports for the United States,* 1992.
40. Marc Mauer, "Young Black Men and the Criminal Justice System," 1990; *LA Times,* 10 October 1995 (Update).
41. Thomas More, *Utopia,* (New York: Washington Square Press, 1965), 10-11.
42. U.S. Bureau of the Census.
43. *LA Times,* 19 December 1992.
44. Ibid.
45. Ibid.
46. *Gregg* v. *Georgia,* 428 U.S. 153 (U.S. Sup. Ct. 1976).
47. U.S. Department of Justice, Bureau of Justice Statistics, 1992.
48. "Capital Punishment, Cruel and Unusual?" Information Series on Current Topics, Wylie, Texas.
49. *The San Diego Union-Tribune,* 22 April 1992.
50. Ibid.
51. Ibid.

52. James Q. Wilson, loc. cit., 138-139.
53. Ibid., 136-137.
54. U.S. Bureau of the Census, 1994.
55. James Q. Wilson, loc. cit., 168.
56. The Holy Bible, New Testament, New International Version, *6 Luke 29* (Grand Rapids, MI: Zondervan Bible Publishers, 1978).
57. Allan B. Chinen, loc. ct., 95.
58. Information Series on Current Topics, op. cit.
59. U.S. Department. of Justice, Bureau of Justice Statistics, 1992.
60. Ibid.
61. Amnesty International, January 1991. The death penalty for non-wartime crimes was abolished by the United Kingdom in 1973 and by Canada in 1976. France abolished the death penalty for all crimes in 1981.
62. Information Series on Current Topics, op. cit.
63. Judith Ahronheim and Doron Weber, *Final Passages,* (New York: Simon & Schuster, 1992), 74.
64. *LA Times,* 5 December 1993.
65. *The San Diego Union Tribune,* 15 June 1993.
66. Derek Humphrey, *Dying with Dignity,* (Carol Publishing Group, 1992), 122.
67. *LA Times,* 21 November 1993.
68. Derek Humphrey, loc. cit., 70.
69. "The Physician and the Hopelessly Ill Patient", Society for the Right to Die (1985), 5-14, 39.
70. *Re Quinlan,* 355 A.2d 647 (New Jersey Sup. Ct. 1976).
71. *Cruzan v. Harmon* Mo. 760 S.W. 2d 408, 1988, 58 LW 4916 (1990).
72. *Roe v. Wade,* op. cit.
73. U.S. Constitution, *Fifth Amendment* (1791), *Fourteenth Amendment* (1868).

## PERMISSIONS

*Grateful acknowledgment is given to the following for permission to reprint copyrighted material:*

Passage from *Dying With Dignity* by Derek Humphry. Copyright 1992 by Derek Humphrey. Reprinted by permission of Carol Publishing Group.

Passage from *Once upon a MidLife* by Allan B. Chinen. Copyright 1992 by Allen B. Chinen. Reprinted by permission of the Putnam Publishing Group/Jeremy P. Tarcher, Inc.

Passages from *Memories, Dreams, Reflections,* by Carl Jung, Copyright 1963 by Random House, Inc. Reprinted by permission of Pantheon Books.

Passage from *A Little Book on the Human Shadow,* by Robert Bly. Copyright 1988 by Robert Bly. Reprinted by permission of Harper Collins Publishers.

Excerpts from *People Of The Lie* by M. Scott Peck, M.D. Copyright 1983 by M. Scott Peck, M.D. Reprinted by permission of Simon & Schuster, Inc.

Excerpts from *The Moral Sense* by James Q. Wilson. Copyright 1993 by James Q. Wilson. Reprinted by permission of The Free Press, a division of Simon & Schuster, Inc.

Passages from *The Sacrament of Abortion* by Ginette Paris. Copyright 1992 by Spring Publications, Inc. Reprinted by permission of the author.

Excerpts from article on Robert Alton Harris with photo from *The Los Angeles Times*, 22 April 1992. Reprinted by permission of The Los Angeles Times Syndicate.

Photograph of Dr. Kevorkian by Steve Liss. Reprinted by permission of Time Magazine, Inc.